IMPACT
SOCIAL STUDIES

Our Place in the World

INQUIRY JOURNAL

Mc
Graw
Hill

Program Authors

James Banks, Ph.D.
University of Washington
Seattle, Washington

Kevin P. Colleary, Ed.D.
Fordham University
New York, New York

William Deverell, Ph.D.
University of Southern California
Los Angeles, California

Daniel Lewis, Ph.D.
The Huntington Library
Los Angeles, California

Elizabeth Logan Ph.D., J.D.
USC Institute on California and the West
Los Angeles, California

Walter C. Parker, Ph.D.
University of Washington
Seattle, Washington

Emily M. Schell, Ed.D.
San Diego State University
San Diego, California

mheducation.com/prek-12

Send all inquiries to:
McGraw-Hill Education
120 S. Riverside Plaza, Suite 1200
Chicago, IL 60606

ISBN: 978-0-07-691564-4
MHID: 0-07-691564-6

Printed in the United States of America.

7 8 9 10 LWI 24 23 22 21

D

Program Consultants

Tahira DuPree Chase, Ed.D.
Greenburgh Central School District
Hartsdale, New York

Jana Echevarria, Ph.D.
California State University
Long Beach, California

Douglas Fisher, Ph.D.
San Diego State University
San Diego, California

Nafees Khan, Ph.D.
Clemson University
Clemson, South Carolina

Jay McTighe
McTighe & Associates Consulting
Columbia, Maryland

Carlos Ulloa, Ed.D.
Escondido Union School District
Escondido, California

Rebecca Valbuena, M.Ed.
Glendora Unified School District
Glendora, California

Program Reviewers

Gary Clayton, Ph.D.
Northern Kentucky University
Highland Heights, Kentucky

Lorri Glover, Ph.D.
Saint Louis University
St. Louis, Missouri

Thomas Herman, Ph.D.
San Diego State University
San Diego, California

Clifford Trafzer, Ph.D.
University of California
Riverside, California

Letter from the Authors

Dear Social Studies Detective,

Think about the world around you. Where do you live? What makes your community and the people who live in it special? What makes you special? In this book, you will find out how many different people make one big nation!

As you read, be an investigator. What do you wonder about? Write your questions. Then look for the answers while you read. What interests and excites you? Take notes about it. Then use your notes to do a project. Share what you learned! Take a closer look at photos of real people and places. Use maps to find your way!

Enjoy your investigation into the amazing world of social studies—a world where each person is special, and each person has a place!

Sincerely,
The IMPACT Social Studies Authors

Japanese American children in school in the 1940s

Contents

Reference Sources

Being a Good Citizen

 What Are the Rights and Responsibilities of Citizens?

Chapter 2

Our Community

ESSENTIAL EQ QUESTION

How Can We Describe Where We Live?

Chapter 3

Celebrating America

 How Do We Celebrate Our Country?

Past and Present

How Does the Past Shape Our Lives?

Chapter 5

People and Money

 EQ **Why Do People Work?**

Skills and Features

Inquiry and Analysis Skills

Reader's Theater

My Notes

Getting Started

You have two social studies books that you will use together to explore and analyze important social studies issues.

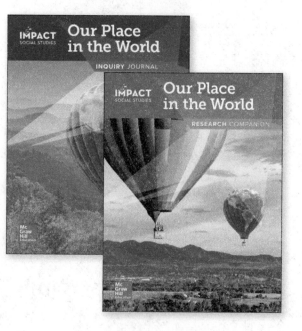

The Inquiry Journal

The Inquiry Journal is your reporter's notebook where you will ask questions, analyze sources, and record information.

The Research Companion

The Research Companion is where you'll read nonfiction and literature selections, examine primary source materials, and look for answers to your questions.

Every Chapter

Chapter opener pages help you see the big picture. Each chapter begins with an **Essential Question**. This **EQ** guides research and inquiry.

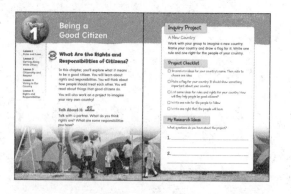

In the **Research Companion**, you'll explore the EQ through words and photographs.

In the **Inquiry Journal**, you'll talk about the EQ and find out about the EQ Inquiry Project for the chapter.

Explore Words

Find out what you know about the chapter's academic vocabulary.

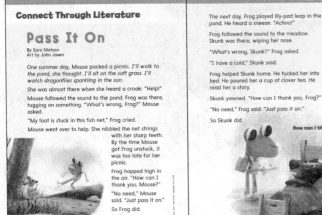

Connect Through Literature

Explore the chapter topic through fiction, informational text, and poetry.

People You Should Know

Learn about the lives of people who have made an impact in history.

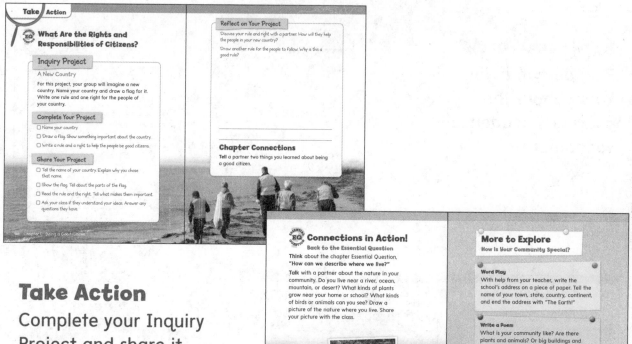

What Are the Rights and Responsibilities of Citizens?

Inquiry Project

A New Country

For this project, your group will imagine a new country. Name your country and draw a flag for it. Write one rule and one right for the people of your country.

Complete Your Project

☐ Name your country.

☐ Draw a flag. Show something important about the country.

☐ Write a rule and a right to help the people be good citizens.

Share Your Project

☐ Tell the name of your country. Explain why you chose that name.

☐ Show the flag. Tell about the parts of the flag.

☐ Read the rule and the right. Tell what makes them important.

☐ Ask your class if they understand your ideas. Answer any questions they have.

Reflect on Your Project

Discuss your rule and right with a partner. How will they help the people in your new country?

Draw another rule for the people to follow. Why is this a good rule?

Chapter Connections

Tell a partner two things you learned about being a good citizen.

Take Action

Complete your Inquiry Project and share it with your class. Then take time to talk about and think about your project. What did you learn?

EQ Connections in Action!

Back to the Essential Question

Think about the chapter Essential Question, "How can we describe where we live?"

Talk with a partner about the nature in your community. Do you live near a river, ocean, mountain, or desert? What kinds of plants grow near your home or school? What kinds of birds or animals can you see? Draw a picture of the nature where you live. Share your picture with the class.

More to Explore

How Is Your Community Special?

Word Play

With help from your teacher, write the school's address on a piece of paper. Tell the name of your town, state, country, continent, and end the address with "The Earth!"

Write a Poem

What is your community like? Are there plants and animals? Or big buildings and many people? List what is special about your community. Pick some words and write them in a poem. Share your poem with others!

Make a Map

Think about your favorite place to visit in your community. How do you get there? Draw a map to show how to find your favorite place.

Chapter 2 87

Connections in Action

Think about the people, places, and events you read about in the chapter. Does this change how you think about the EQ? Talk with a partner about it.

Every Lesson

Lesson Question lets you think about how the lesson connects to the chapter EQ.

Lesson Outcomes help you think about what you will be learning and how it applies to the EQ.

Images and text provide opportunities to explore the lesson topic.

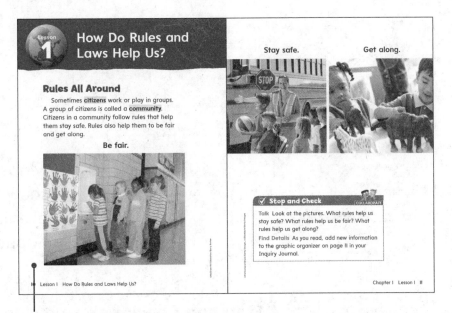

Lesson selections help you develop a deeper understanding of the lesson topic and the EQ.

Analyze and Inquire

The **Inquiry Journal** provides the tools you need to analyze a source. You'll use those tools to investigate the texts in the **Research Companion** and use the graphic organizer in the **Inquiry Journal** to organize your findings.

Inquiry Tools help you analyze and explore.

Graphic Organizers help you organize information as you read.

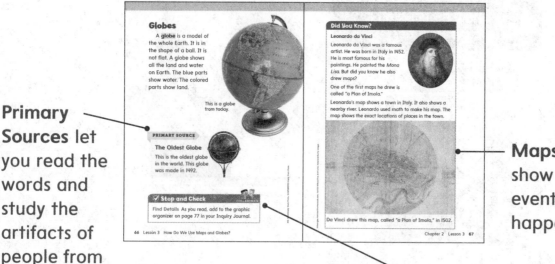

Primary Sources let you read the words and study the artifacts of people from the past and present.

Maps show where events happened.

Stop and Check boxes provide opportunities to check your understanding, consider different perspectives, and make connections.

Report Your Findings

At the end of each lesson, you have an opportunity in the **Inquiry Journal** to report your findings and connect back to the EQ. In the Research Companion, you'll think about the lesson focus question.

Think about what you have learned.

Write about it using text evidence to support your ideas.

Connect to the EQ.

Think about what you read in the lesson. How does this give you a new understanding about the lesson focus question?

What Are the Rights and Responsibilities of Citizens?

In this chapter, you'll explore what it means to be a good citizen. You will learn about rights and responsibilities. You will think about how people should treat each other. You will read about things that good citizens do.

You will also work on a project to imagine your very own country!

Talk About It

Talk with a partner. What do you think rights are? What are some responsibilities you have?

Inquiry Project

A New Country

Work with your group to imagine a new country. Name your country and draw a flag for it. Write one rule and one right for the people of your country.

Project Checklist

☐ Brainstorm ideas for your country's name. Then vote to choose one idea.

☐ Make a flag for your country. It should show something important about your country.

☐ List some ideas for rules and rights for your country. How will they help people be good citizens?

☐ Write one rule for the people to follow.

☐ Write one right that the people will have.

My Research Ideas

What questions do you have about the project?

1. _____

_____

2. _____

_____

Explore Words

Complete this chapter's Word Rater. Write notes as you learn more about each word.

citizen   My Notes
- ☐ Know It!   _____
- ☐ Heard It!
- ☐ Don't Know It!   _____

community   My Notes
- ☐ Know It!   _____
- ☐ Heard It!
- ☐ Don't Know It!   _____

democracy   My Notes
- ☐ Know It!   _____
- ☐ Heard It!
- ☐ Don't Know It!   _____

law   My Notes
- ☐ Know It!   _____
- ☐ Heard It!
- ☐ Don't Know It!   _____

past   My Notes
- ☐ Know It!   _____
- ☐ Heard It!
- ☐ Don't Know It!   _____

respect

My Notes

☐ Know It!

☐ Heard It! _____

☐ Don't Know It! _____

responsibility My Notes

☐ Know It!

☐ Heard It! _____

☐ Don't Know It! _____

rights

My Notes

☐ Know It! _____

☐ Heard It!

☐ Don't Know It! _____

voting

My Notes

☐ Know It! _____

☐ Heard It!

☐ Don't Know It! _____

Lesson Outcomes

What Am I Learning?
You will explore how rules and laws help us.

Why Am I Learning It?
You will learn how rules and laws help groups of people live together.

How Will I Know that I Learned It?
You will list rules and laws that help people stay safe and work together.

Talk About It
COLLABORATE

Look closely at the student. What is she doing? What rules is she following?

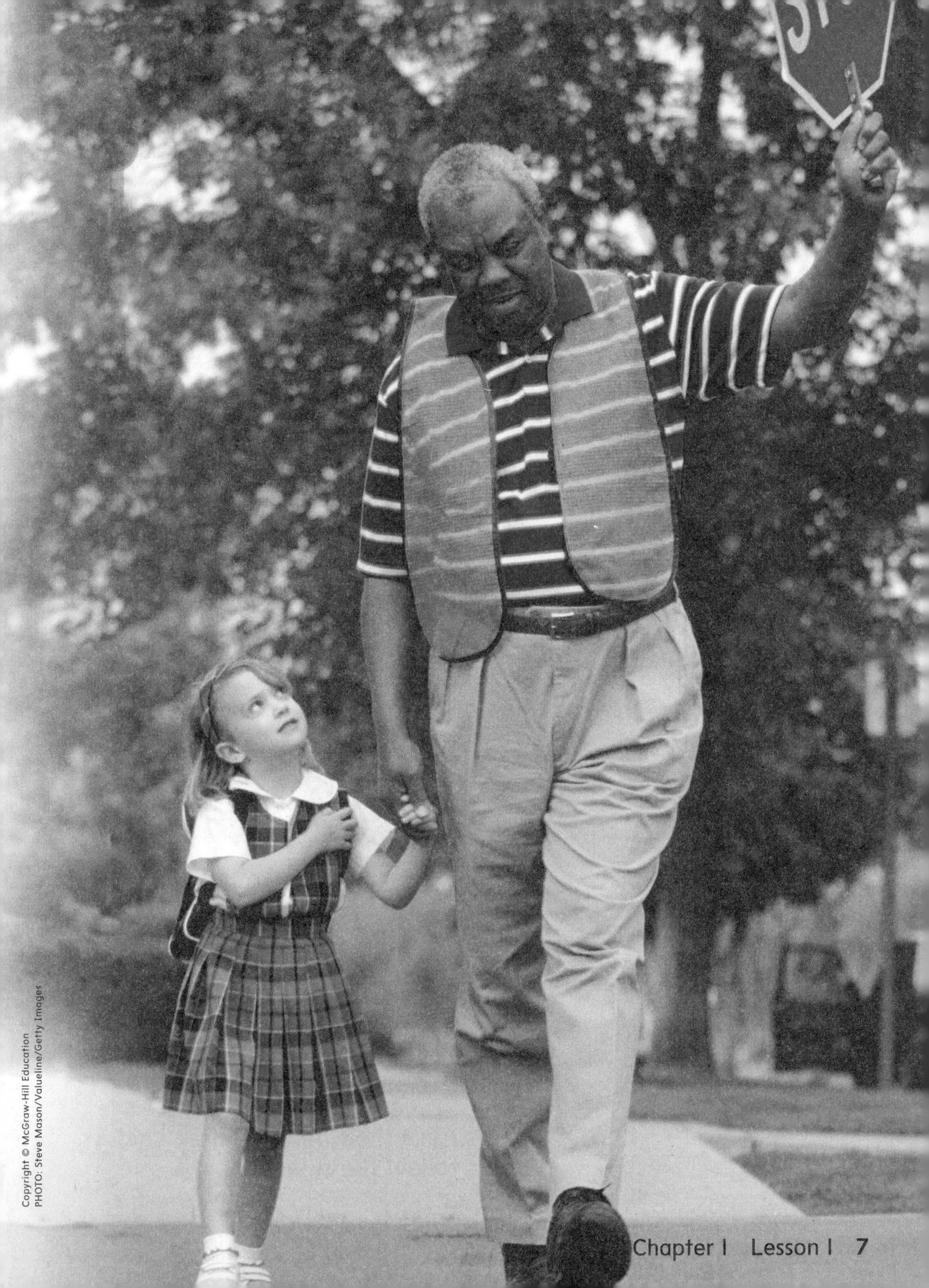
ST

What Are Rules?

Read Look at the title. What do you think this text will be about?

Circle words you don't know.

Underline clues that tell you:

• Why do we have rules?
• Who follows rules?

My Notes

_____

_____

_____

_____

Rules tell us what to do. Rules help us stay safe. Rules help us get along.

One rule is to walk when you are inside. This rule keeps people safe. It is not safe to run inside.

Good citizens follow rules. **Citizens** are people in a group. Citizens work or play together.

Rules help us have fun. Rules help us get jobs done. It is good for citizens to follow rules.

Students raise their hands to talk in class. Students follow the rules.

Students are citizens of a classroom. Students follow class rules. One rule is to always put trash in the trash can. This rule keeps the room clean.

Students share computers and other tools. Sharing is an important rule. Sharing helps everyone get a turn.

The rules in your class help students learn and work together.

More people get to use classroom supplies when they are shared.

2 Find Evidence

Reread Why do people follow rules?

Underline clues that tell why people follow rules.

3 Make Connections

Talk Turn back to page 7. How are the people in this picture being good citizens? What rules are they following? Why are these rules important?

COLLABORATE

Explore Topic and Key Details

The **main topic** is what the text is about.

Key details tell you more about the main topic.

To find the main topic and key details:

1. Read the whole text. What is it about?
   This is the **main topic**.

2. Reread the text.

3. Look for sentences that tell you about the main topic.
   These are **key details**.

 Work with your class to complete
the chart.

Main Topic: Rules	
Key Detail Good citizens follow the rules.	**Key Detail**

Investigate!

Read pages 10–15 in your Research Companion.

Look for key details about rules and laws.

Write your information in the graphic organizer.

Main Topic: Rules and Laws	
Key Detail	**Key Detail**
Rules and laws help citizens _____ and _____.	

Think About It

Think about what you read. What are rules?
Why are rules important?

Write About It

Think of a rule you read about.
Why do you think the rule is important?

One important rule is

_____

_____

Draw a picture to show the rule.

Talk About It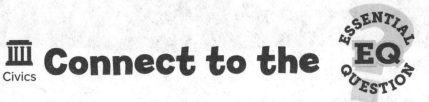

Share your work with a partner.
Tell about the rule.

Connect to the EQ

Civics

List two rules that you follow at school.

1. _____

2. _____

Inquiry Project Notes

_____

_____

_____

_____

_____

Lesson 2

How Can We Get Along With Each Other?

Lesson Outcomes

What Am I Learning?

You will explore how people solve problems and reach fair decisions.

Why Am I Learning It?

You will see how people find ways to work together and get along.

How Will I Know that I Learned it?

You will suggest different ways for people to solve problems and agree with each other.

Talk About It COLLABORATE

Look closely at the picture. What are they doing? Are they getting along well together? How do you know?

Read Look at the pictures. What do you think this selection will be about?

Circle words you don't know.

Underline clues that tell you:

- What makes people disagree?
- What happens when they disagree?

My Notes

_____

_____

_____

Good Citizens Get Along Together

People don't always have the same ideas. When people disagree, they talk about it. They share ideas. They find a way to do things that makes everyone happy. They find ways to agree.

Children can help each other. They can share things like toys. They can teach each other new skills, like how to skate or ride a bike. Children can help their classmates solve problems.

People share, and people help each other get along.

The classroom is messy. It needs to be cleaned up. The desks must be cleared. The books need to be put on the shelves.

The teacher splits up the work. One group clears the desks. The other group puts books away. Everyone helps. When everyone helps, people get along.

Splitting up the work helps everyone get along.

2 Find Evidence
Reread What do the pictures show you about people getting along?

Draw a box around the words that tell how people get along.

3 Make Connections
Talk Look back at the text on page 16. What problems can children solve together?

Explore Problem and Solution

A **problem** is something that goes wrong and needs to be fixed.

A **solution** is the way a person solves or fixes the problem.

To find the problem and solution:

1. Read the whole text.

2. Look for something wrong that needs to be fixed. This is the problem. Circle it.

3. Underline the sentences that show how the problem is fixed. This is the solution.

4. Ask yourself, *Does the solution make sense? Does it fix the problem?*

 Work with your class to fill in the chart.

Problem	Solution
The classroom is very messy and needs to be cleaned up.	

Investigate!

Read pages 16–23 in your Research Companion.

Look for details about problems and their solutions.

Write the details you find in the chart.

Problem	Solution
Two goats want to cross the bridge at the same time. There is not enough room.	
	Amy and Chamara take turns and work together.

Think About It

Think about the different ways people get along.
Can you name two ways?

Write About It

What is one good way to get along with others?
Use an example from what you read.

One way to get along is to _____

_____

_____

_____

Draw a picture of people getting along.

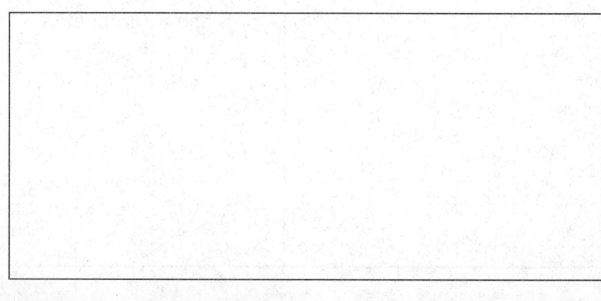

Talk About It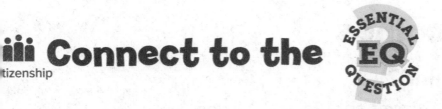

Share your work with a partner. Talk together about ways to get along in the classroom.

tizenship

Connect to the EQ

Read about the problems below. Work with a partner. Discuss a solution for each problem.

1. Three children want to color in red, but there is only one red crayon.

2. One of your classmates is angry or upset.

Inquiry Project Notes

_____

_____

_____

_____

_____

Lesson Outcomes

What Am I Learning?
You will explore how citizens should treat each other and how to be fair.

Why Am I Learning it?
You will know how a person can help others.

How Will I Know that I Learned it?
You will list things you could do to help others in your community.

Talk About It COLLABORATE

Look closely at the picture. What are the boys doing? Would it be fun to play on their team? Why?

Games are more fun
when we help each other.

1 Inspect

Read Look at the title. What do you think this text will be about?

Circle words you don't know.

Underline clues that tell you:

- What does respect mean?
- How do we show respect?
- What are you thinking about when you show respect?

My Notes

_____

_____

_____

Respect Everyone

How should people treat each other? We help each other. We take turns and share. We play fair. When we do this, we show **respect**. Respect means being polite. It means thinking about how another person feels. Respect is being kind. It is being fair.

These students are working together. They are showing respect to each other and to Earth.

Children have the right to go to school. Students respect each other's rights by being kind.

We respect people's **rights**. Rights are things that people are free to do. Everyone has the right to speak out. Everyone has the right to be treated fairly and with respect. People come from many places. They can be young or old. They can be big or small. They can be the same as others or different from others. We respect everyone's rights.

2 Find Evidence

Reread How does the text describe differences between people?

Underline the right that everyone has.

3 Make Connections

Talk Why are games more fun when we respect each other?

Look back at the picture on page 23. How are the students showing respect for each other?

Explore Words and Pictures

You learn details from the **words** and the **pictures** in a text.

To use words and pictures:

1. Read the title. The title tells what the text is about.

2. Look at the pictures. How do they add to the text?

3. Read the captions. The caption is the sentence under the picture.

 Based on the words and pictures, work with your class to complete the chart.

Page Number	What I Learn from the Words	What I Learn from the Pictures
24	It is important to respect people.	
25		Children have the right to go to school.

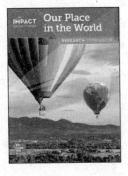

Investigate!

Read pages 24-29 in your Research Companion.

Look for clues from the words and pictures.

Write your notes in this chart.

Page Number	What I Learn from the Words	What I Learn from the Pictures
26	The Golden Rule tells us to treat people as we would like to be treated.	
29		People work together to build homes.

Think About It

Think about what you have read. Then think about how you can treat others with respect.

Draw It

How can people help others and show respect? Draw a picture of a person helping others in the school or community. Write a label for your picture.

Talk About It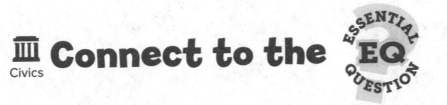

Share your drawing with a partner. Talk about other ways to help people and show respect.

Civics Connect to the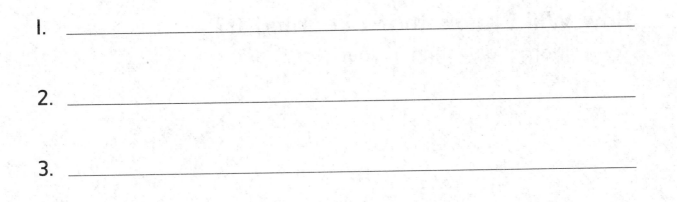

How can you be a good citizen? List three things you could do to be a good citizen in your community.

1. _____

2. _____

3. _____

   _____

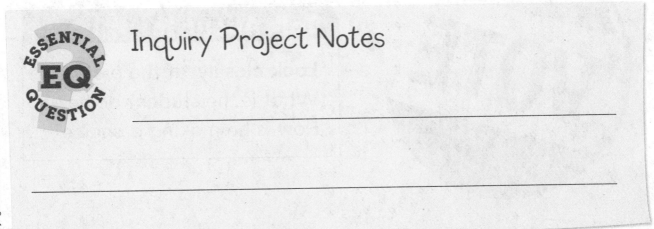

Inquiry Project Notes

_____

_____

Why Do We Vote?

Lesson Outcomes

What Am I Learning?
You will explore voting and why people vote.

Why Am I Learning It?
You will know why voting is important.

How Will I Know that I Learned It?
You will practice voting in your classroom.

Talk About It COLLABORATE

Look closely at the picture.
What is the student doing?
How is he making a choice?

These students wrote their votes on paper.

BALLOT BOX

1 Inspect

Read Look at the title. What do you think this text will be about?

Circle words you don't know.

Underline clues that tell you:

- What is voting?
- How can people vote?
- Why do people vote?

My Notes

_____

_____

_____

_____

Voting Matters

Voting is making a choice that can be counted. Voting is a way to be fair. Everybody gets a chance to say what they want.

A class wants to name their pet hamster. The choices are Fluffy and Doodle. Each student chooses the name he or she likes best. Each choice is one vote. The pet name with the most votes wins.

These students vote in their classroom.

There are many ways to vote. People can vote in public. They can raise their hands or say their choice.

When Americans vote for leaders, the votes are private. Americans don't have to tell others who they voted for. Voting is important. Voting is a way that citizens choose leaders fairly.

A voting booth keeps votes private. Others can't see who we choose.

2 Find Evidence

Compare How do the two pictures show the same kind of voting?

Underline the text that tells how this kind of voting is done in America.

3 Make Connections

Talk Good citizens vote for their leaders. Why do you think this is important? Why is it important for you to vote in your classroom?

COLLABORATE

Explore Topic and Key Details

The **topic** is what the text is about.

Key details tell you about the topic of a text.

You can use words and pictures to learn key details.

To find the topic and key details:

1. Read the whole text. Decide what the text is about. This is the topic.

2. Look for sentences about the topic. These are key details.

3. Look at the words, pictures, and captions. Underline the key details.

4. Ask yourself, *Do these details tell me important things about the main topic?*

COLLABORATE Work with your class to complete the chart.

Main Topic: Voting Is Important	
Key Detail	Key Detail
Voting is a way to be fair.	

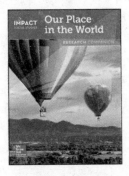

Investigate!

Read pages 30-35 in your Research Companion.

Look for key details about why voting is important.

Write the information in the chart.

Main Topic: Voting Is Important	
Key Detail	**Key Detail**
Voting gives everyone an _____ say.	

Think About It

Think about what you have read.
Why do people vote?

Write About It

What is voting?

_____

_____

_____

_____

List two things people can choose by voting.

1. _____

2. _____

Talk About It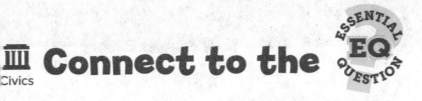

Share your response with a partner. Together, discuss some choices the class could make together by voting.

Connect to the EQ

Civics

Take a vote. What supplies does your classroom need? As a group, write three things the classroom needs. Then take a class-wide vote. Record the results in a bar graph.

How Have Rights and Responsibilities Changed Over Time?

Lesson Outcomes

What Am I Learning?

You will explore rights and responsibilities of the past.

Why Am I Learning It?

You will know how responsibilities and rights have changed over time.

How Will I Know that I Learned It?

You will list rights and responsibilities today that are different from the past.

Talk About It

COLLABORATE

Look closely at the picture. What responsibilities do these children have when they are in school?

1 Inspect

Read Look at the pictures. What do you think this text will be about?

Circle the details that tell you who the text is about.

Highlight the sentences that tell you:

- What did the person do?
- What responsibilities did the person have?

My Notes

_____

_____

_____

Booker T. Washington

Booker T. Washington was born long ago. His mother was an enslaved woman. In the **past**, many African Americans were enslaved. They had few rights. They were forced to do hard work for other people. Later, African Americans became free citizens. But they still did not have equal rights.

Washington became a free citizen when he was a boy. He went to a school for African American students. He worked at the school to pay the cost. He did very well. Then he became a teacher.

Booker T. Washington was a teacher and a leader.

Washington wanted to help others. He became the leader of a new school. It was for African Americans. They were not allowed to go to schools with white students. Washington helped his students learn many skills. Some of the students became teachers. The school grew and grew.

Today, African Americans have the right to go to any school in the United States. And many of those schools are named for Booker T. Washington.

Booker T. Washington helped African American teachers and students.

2 Find Evidence

Reread How did Booker T. Washington's rights and responsibilities change?

Underline the words that show these rights and responsibilities.

3 Make Connections

Draw
Look at the pictures on these pages. Draw your own picture of Booker T. Washington teaching students.

COLLABORATE

Explore Contrast

When you **contrast**, you think about how things are different.

To contrast details in the text:

1. Read the whole text.

2. Reread the text. Circle words that tell you how things were in the past.

3. Reread the text again. Underline words that tell you how things are today.

 Read the text. Then work with your class to complete the chart.

In the Past	Today
	African Americans have the right to go to any school in the United States.

Investigate!

Read pages 36–41 in your Research Companion.

Look for details that tell you about how rights and responsibilities have changed.

Write the details in the chart.

In the Past	Today
	Children can go to school.
People had responsibilities like chopping wood and getting water.	

Think About It

Think about children's lives in the past. How have children's rights and responsibilities changed?

Write About It

Work with a partner to complete the sentences. Use details from the texts to help you complete the sentences.

One responsibility children had in the past was _____

_____

_____

_____

One right children have today is _____

_____

_____

_____

_____

Talk About It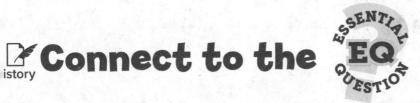

Discuss with your partner how rights and responsibilities have changed over time.

Connect to the EQ

List three ways rights and responsibilities have changed from the past.

1. _____

   _____

2. _____

   _____

3. _____

   _____

Take Action

EQ
ESSENTIAL QUESTION

What Are the Rights and Responsibilities of Citizens?

Inquiry Project

A New Country

For this project, your group will imagine a new country. Name your country and draw a flag for it. Write one rule and one right for the people of your country.

Complete Your Project

☐ Name your country.

☐ Draw a flag. Show something important about the country.

☐ Write a rule and a right to help the people be good citizens.

Share Your Project

☐ Tell the name of your country. Explain why you chose that name.

☐ Show the flag. Tell about the parts of the flag.

☐ Read the rule and the right. Tell what makes them important.

☐ Ask your class if they understand your ideas. Answer any questions they have.

Reflect on Your Project

Discuss your rule and right with a partner. How will they help the people in your new country?

Draw another rule for the people to follow. Why is this a good rule?

Chapter Connections

Tell a partner two things you learned about being a good citizen.

Goldilocks and the Three Bears

CHARACTERS

Goldilocks
Mama Bear
Papa Bear
Baby Bear
Narrator
Group A
Group B

Narrator: Goldilocks went to visit the three bears. But they were not home.

Goldilocks: I will go inside and wait for them.

Narrator: Goldilocks went inside.

Groups A and B: Yum! Three bowls of soup!

Goldilocks: Should I eat some of this tasty soup?

Narrator: Goldilocks was hungry. But she wasn't sure about eating the soup.

Narrator: Goldilocks decided to eat a bowl of soup. Then the bears came home!

Papa Bear: Hello, Goldilocks! Sorry we are late.

Mama Bear: Have you been waiting a long time?

Baby Bear: Hey! Someone ate my soup!

Narrator: Baby Bear started to cry.

Goldilocks: I'm sorry, Baby Bear. It was me. I ate your soup.

Mama Bear: You should not take what isn't yours, Goldilocks. That is a rule in this house.

Goldilocks: I'm sorry. I did not know the rule.

Papa Bear: It's okay, Baby Bear, you can have my soup.

Baby Bear: Thanks, Papa!

Goldilocks: I feel bad about eating Baby Bear's soup.

Group A: Do something nice for Baby Bear!

Group B: You should make more soup. That will cheer up Baby Bear!

Goldilocks: Papa Bear, would you teach me how to make soup? I want to make some more.

Papa Bear: That's a good idea, Goldilocks. I will show you how. Then we can all have soup. I hope you learned not to take what isn't yours.

Goldilocks: I sure did. Let's make more soup!

Narrator: They made a big pot of soup and ate it together.

Groups A and B: It was yummy!

Our Community

ESSENTIAL EQ QUESTION

How Can We Describe Where We Live?

In this chapter, you'll explore places in your community and around the world. You'll learn how to find places using a map or globe. You'll discover how one place can be part of many locations. You'll also make a flipbook of where you live!

Talk About It COLLABORATE

Talk about your community with a partner. How can you describe it? What makes it special?

Inquiry Project

Where We Live

Work with your group to create flipbooks. Think and talk about different ways to describe where you live. Write and draw in your own flipbook.

Project Checklist

☐ **Talk** with your group about how to tell where you live. Are you on Earth? Are you in a state?

☐ **Write** one sentence on each page to describe the location of your community. You should have at least four pages.

☐ **Brainstorm** what you will draw on each page. Think about what makes each place different from other places.

☐ **Draw** a picture for each sentence in the flipbook. Show what makes that location special.

My Research Ideas

What questions do you have about the project?

1. _____

_____

2. _____

_____

Explore Words

Complete this chapter's Word Rater. Write notes as you learn more about each word.

address   My Notes

☐ Know It!   _____

☐ Heard It!

☐ Don't Know It!   _____

border   My Notes

☐ Know It!   _____

☐ Heard It!

☐ Don't Know It!   _____

capital   My Notes

☐ Know It!   _____

☐ Heard It!

☐ Don't Know It!   _____

continent   My Notes

☐ Know It!   _____

☐ Heard It!

☐ Don't Know It!   _____

environment   My Notes

☐ Know It!   _____

☐ Heard It!

☐ Don't Know It!   _____

globe   My Notes

☐ Know It!   _____

☐ Heard It!

☐ Don't Know It!   _____

location   My Notes

☐ Know It!   _____

☐ Heard It!

☐ Don't Know It!   _____

neighborhood My Notes

☐ Know It!   _____

☐ Heard It!

☐ Don't Know It!   _____

symbols   My Notes

☐ Know It!   _____

☐ Heard It!

☐ Don't Know It!   _____

transportation My Notes

☐ Know It!   _____

☐ Heard It!

☐ Don't Know It!

Lesson Outcomes

What Am I Learning?
You will explore how maps help us.

Why Am I Learning It?
You will understand how maps show many different places.

How Will I Know that I Learned It?
You will draw a map and list things maps can help us do.

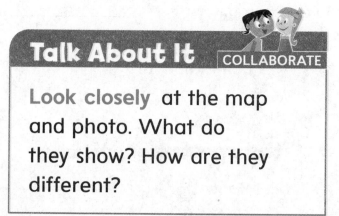

Talk About It   COLLABORATE

Look closely at the map and photo. What do they show? How are they different?

Playground Map

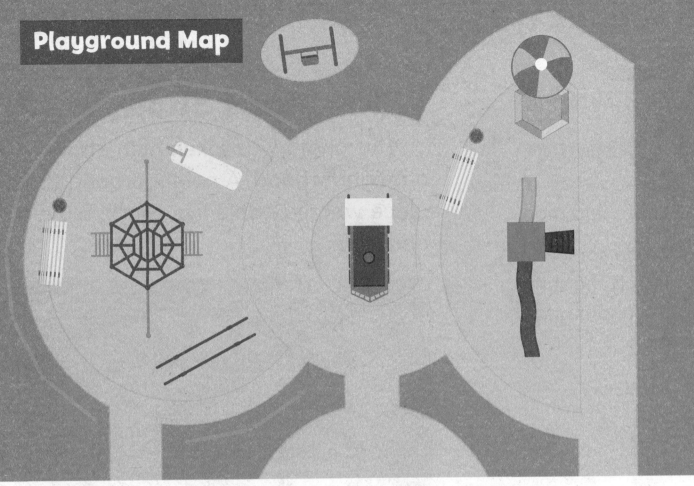

This map shows different places in a playground.

The photo shows places in a real playground.

1 Inspect

Look closely at the photo and map.

Circle something that is the same in the photo and the map.

My Notes

_____

_____

_____

_____

_____

_____

What Maps Show

This photo was taken high above a **neighborhood**. A neighborhood is a place where people live, work, play, and shop.

What places do you see in this neighborhood?

Neighborhood Map

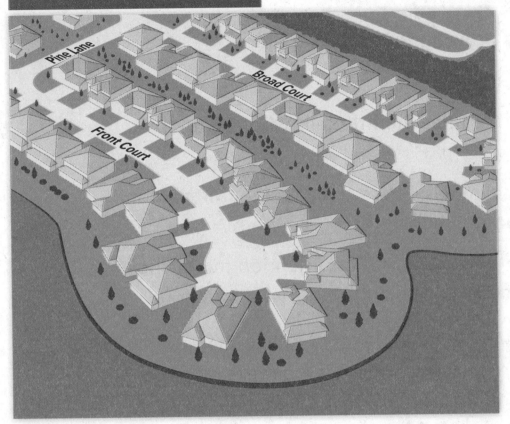

Pine Lane

Broad Court

Front Court

A map shows where places are located. Maps help you know how to get from place to place.

This is a map. It shows the same neighborhood that you see in the photo.

2 Find Evidence

Reread How can a map be more helpful than a photo?

Circle something on the map that is not in the photo.

3 Make Connections

Talk How are the photo and the map alike? How are they different?

Turn back to page 57. How does the map help you understand the playground?

Explore Map Skills

A **map** is a drawing that shows a place.

To read a map:

1. Look at the title. The title tells what the map shows.

2. Look for symbols. These tell you about important places on the map.

3. Look for other information. The map might show street names or buildings.

COLLABORATE Work with your class to fill in the graphic organizer with details from the maps and text.

Map Feature (What You See on a Map)	How It Helps
Street names	

Investigate!

Read pages 52–57 in your Research Companion.

Look for clues that tell you what each feature of a map does.

Write your information in the graphic organizer.

Map Feature (What You See on a Map)	How It Helps
Title	
Label	
Compass rose	
Cardinal directions	
Map key	
Symbol	

Think About It

How would you show places in your school on a map?

Draw It

Draw a map of your school.
Use symbols and a map key. Add a compass rose.

Talk About It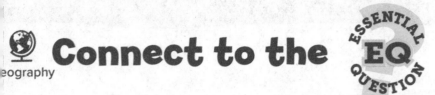

Share your map with a partner. Tell your partner what you drew.

Connect to the EQ ESSENTIAL QUESTION

Geography

List three things that a map can help us do.

1. _____

_____

2. _____

_____

3. _____

_____

_____

What Can We Learn From Different Kinds of Maps?

Lesson Outcomes

What Am I Learning?

You will learn about different kinds of maps.

Why Am I Learning It?

You will know what maps can show us.

How Will I Know that I Learned it?

You will draw a map of your state.

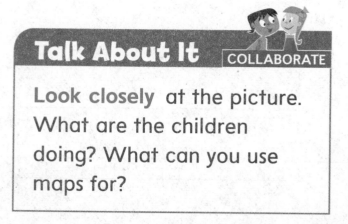

Talk About It COLLABORATE

Look closely at the picture. What are the children doing? What can you use maps for?

Maps can teach us many different things about a place.

1 Inspect

Read Look at the title. What do you think you will learn?

Circle the map key.

Highlight a capital city.

Underline clues that tell you:

- what a political map shows.
- what a capital city is.

My Notes

_____

_____

_____

Political Maps

Political maps show borders of states. They also show borders of countries. **Borders** are the lines around a state or country. They show where one place ends and another begins.

A political map also shows bodies of water. It shows a state's capital city. The **capital** city has state government offices.

This political map shows some of the states in the United States. Some states share a border with Mexico. Some states share a border with Canada.

MAP KEY

★ Capital City

📍 **Map Skills** What are the names of the states that share a border with Iowa?

A political map shows the capital city of a state.

2 Find Evidence

Reread How do borders on a political map help you know more about a state?

Circle the name of the country that is on the border to the south.

3 Make Connections

Talk What states share a border with Missouri?

Explore Key Details

Key details tell you more about a topic.

To find the key details:

1. Read the whole text. It is about one kind of map. This is the topic.

2. Reread the text.

3. Look for sentences that tell you about the topic. These are key details.

 COLLABORATE Work with your class to complete the chart below.

Type of Map	Key Detail About the Map
Political Map	A political map shows the _____ between states and countries.

Investigate!

Read pages 58–63 in your Research Companion.

Look for key details about different types of maps.

Write the details in the chart.

Type of Map	Key Detail About the Map
Physical Map	A physical map shows different types of _____ and _____.
Product Map	A product map shows where things are _____ or _____.
Weather Map	A weather map can use _____ to show what the weather is like.

Think About It

Think about what you read. Why do people use different types of maps?

Draw It

Draw a map of your state. Add the state name and capital city.

Use symbols and a map key to show water and land. What other details can you add?

Talk About It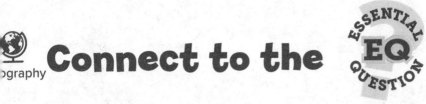

COLLABORATE

Share your map with a partner. Tell your partner what the symbols show.

Connect to the EQ

ESSENTIAL QUESTION

Geography

What can we learn from using different types of maps? Work with a partner. Draw lines to show what type of map you would use to find the information listed below.

Information	Type of Map
Find out where apples are grown.	Weather Map
Find out if it will rain where you live.	Physical Map
Find out the capital city of your state.	Product Map
Find out where a lake is located.	Political Map

How Do We Use Maps and Globes?

Lesson Outcomes

What Am I Learning?

You will learn how maps and globes are alike and different.

Why Am I Learning it?

You will know when to use a map and when to use a globe.

How Will I Know that I Learned it?

You will explain what maps and globes show us about where we live.

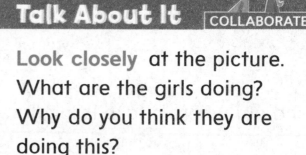

Talk About It   COLLABORATE

Look closely at the picture. What are the girls doing? Why do you think they are doing this?

A globe shows us what Earth looks like.

1 Inspect

Read Look at the pictures. How are they alike? How are they different?

Circle the land and water in both pictures.

Draw arrows to point to things that are in one picture and not in the other.

My Notes

_____

_____

_____

_____

_____

What Is A Globe?

Look at this picture of Earth from space. Then look at the globe on the next page. A **globe** is a model of Earth in the shape of a ball. A globe shows the whole Earth.

This is a picture of Earth from space.

The picture of Earth shows land and water. It also shows clouds. The globe uses different colors to show land. Each country is shown in a different color.

The globe also shows the equator. The equator is an imaginary line around the middle of Earth.

2 Find Evidence

Look What can you learn about Earth from a globe?

Underline words that teach you about Earth.

3 Make Connections

Talk How are the picture of Earth and the globe alike? How are they different?

COLLABORATE

A globe shows the equator.

Explore Compare and Contrast

When you **compare**, you think about how things are alike.

When you **contrast**, you think about how things are different.

To compare and contrast:

1. Read the whole text.

2. Circle words that tell you how things are alike.

3. Underline words that tell you how things are different.

COLLABORATE Work with your class to complete the graphic organizer below.

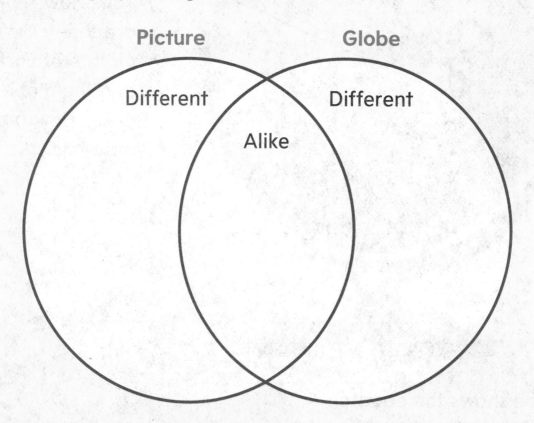

Picture   Globe

Different   Different

Alike

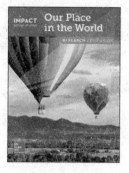

Investigate!

Read pages 64–69 in your Research Companion.

Look for clues that tell you how maps and globes are alike and different.

Write your information in the graphic organizer.

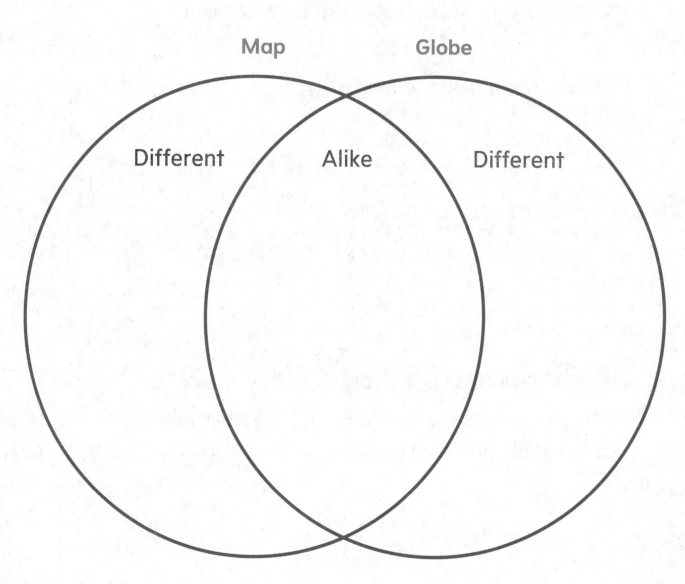

Map   Globe

Different   Alike   Different

Think About It

Think about what you read. How do globes and maps help us understand location?

Write About It

When would you use a globe? When would you use a map?

Tell about a time you would use each of them.

I would use a globe to look at _____

_____

I would use a map to look at _____

_____

Talk About It COLLABORATE

Share your response with a group. Together talk about what you learned about maps and globes.

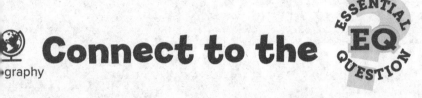

Connect to the EQ

ESSENTIAL QUESTION

Should I Use a Map or a Globe?

Your friend wants to find the city library. Should she use a map or a globe? Draw a picture of the one she should use. Then explain why she should use that one.

_____

_____

_____

Where Is Our Community in the World?

Lesson **4**

Lesson Outcomes

What Am I Learning?
You will explore different ways to locate and talk about your community.

Why Am I Learning it?
You will be able to show and tell where your community is located.

How Will I Know that I Learned it?
You will describe your community and explain where it is located.

Talk About It COLLABORATE

Look closely at the photos. What are the children doing? How do you know?

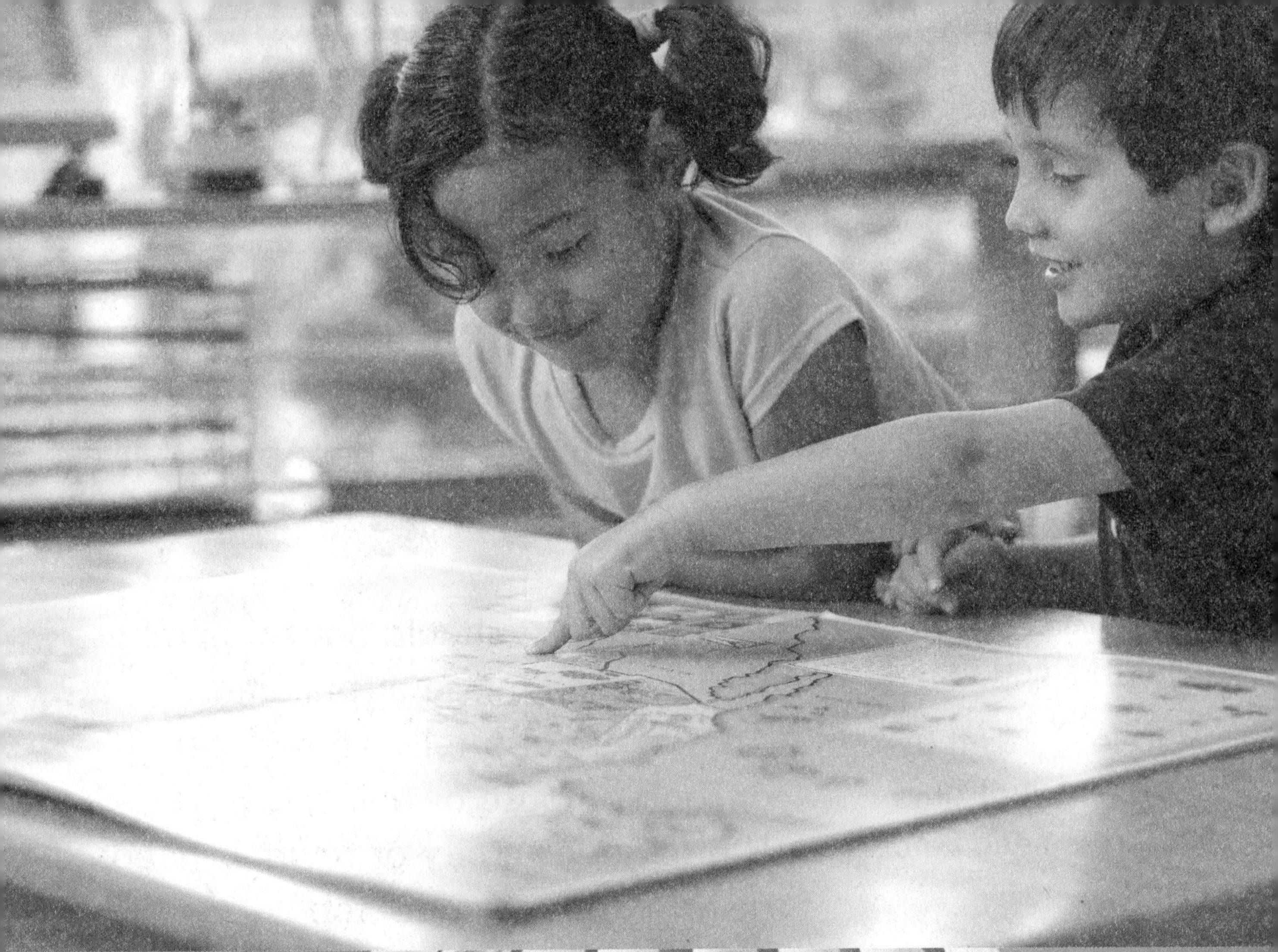

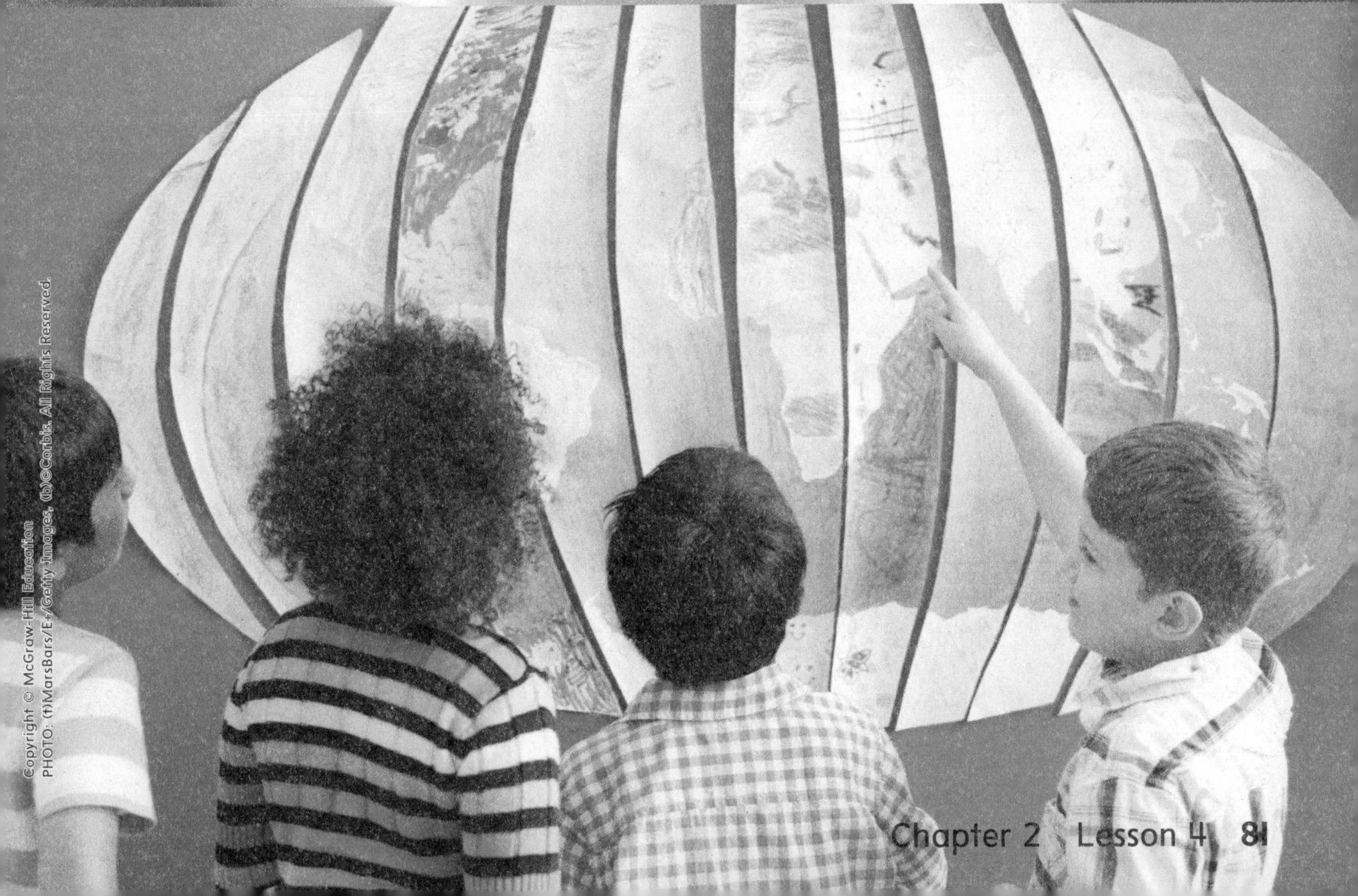

1 Inspect

Read Look at the title. What do you think this text will be about?

Underline words that explain what an address can tell us.

Circle words that explain what an address needs to show.

My Notes

_____

_____

_____

_____

My Address

It's fun to get a card in the mail! How does the card get to you? The sender needs to know your address.

An **address** tells where people live or work. An address gives an exact **location**.

An address should have a number to tell which house or building. An address also tells what street or road a house or building is on. It also needs a city or town. It needs a state and zip code, too.

Lin Potts
316 Elm Street
Apt. B-5
Eugene, OR 97402

OR is a short way to write *Oregon*.

Jack is sending cards to his friends. He wrote each name on the first line of the address. That tells who the card is for.

The next line tells the house or building number. It tells the street each friend lives on. Kaylie's address has her apartment number, too.

The last line tells the name of the city or town. It also tells the state and the zip code.

Marita Lee
600 Park Street
Ann Arbor, MI 48105

Ben Jackson
152 Hill Road
Lancaster, PA 17602

Kaylie Boyle
7522 Channel Ave., Apt. 4
Topeka, KS 66546

The parts of an address tell postal workers where to deliver mail.

2 Find Evidence

Reread How do the pictures help you understand the parts of an address?

Underline the street name, town, and state for each address.

3 Make Connections

Talk Why is each part of an address important? What might happen if you forgot to write part of an address?

Inquiry Tools

Explore Main Topic and Key Details

The **main topic** is what the text is about.

Key details give information about the main topic.

To find the main topic and key details:

1. Read the title and the text.

2. Ask yourself: *Does the title give a clue about the main topic?*

3. Decide what the text is about. This is the main topic. Circle it.

4. Look for details that give information about the main topic. Underline two or three key details.

COLLABORATE Work with your class to complete the graphic organizer below.

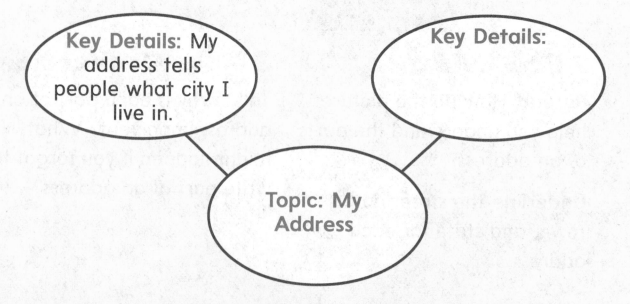

Key Details: My address tells people what city I live in.

Key Details:

Topic: My Address

Copyright © McGraw-Hill Education

Investigate!

Read pages 70–77 in your Research Companion.

Look for key details about communities and where your community is located.

Write your information in the graphic organizer.

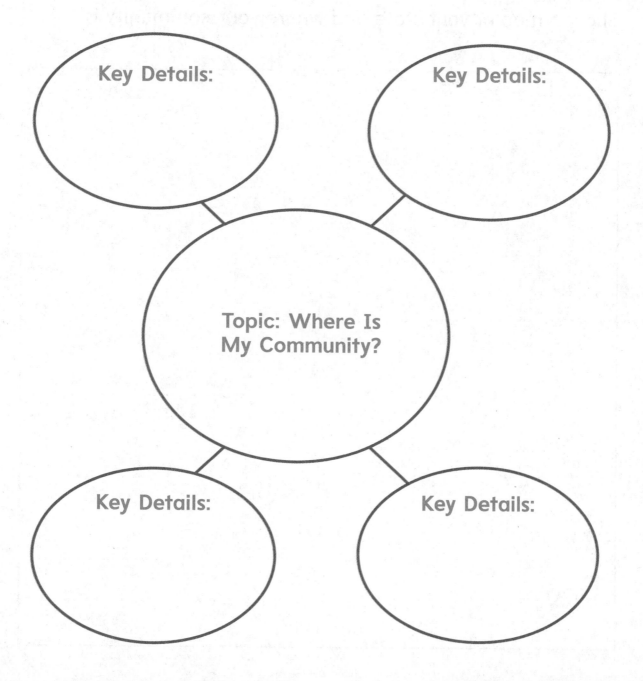

Key Details:

Key Details:

Topic: Where Is My Community?

Key Details:

Key Details:

Think About It

Think about what you just read about communities. Where is your community?

Draw It

Draw a picture to show where your community is located. Show a map of your state and where your community is.

Talk About It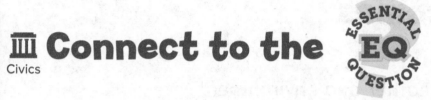

Share your picture with a partner. Talk about what your community is like. Where is it located? How is it different from other communities?

🏛 Connect to the ESSENTIAL EQ QUESTION

Civics

Complete the three sentences to describe your community.

1. The name of my community is _____

_____ .

2. My community is located _____

_____ .

3. My community is special because _____

_____ .

How Do Location and Weather Affect Us?

Lesson Outcomes

What Am I Learning?
You will learn about weather and environment in different places.

Why Am I Learning It?
You will understand more about the weather in your own community.

How Will I Know that I Learned It?
You will draw and write about how location and weather affect life in your community.

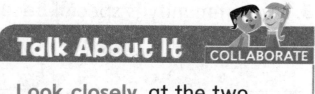

Talk About It COLLABORATE

Look closely at the two pictures. What do you think the weather is like in each place? How do you know?

1 Inspect

Read Look at the title and picture captions. What do you think this text will be about?

Circle words you don't know.

Underline the differences between the environments.

My Notes

_____

_____

_____

_____

_____

How We Live

A location is a place. Different locations have different environments. An **environment** is the nature that surrounds a living thing. Is your community near the ocean or the mountains? Maybe it is near a forest or a desert.

The environment also affects how people live. Food, clothes, homes, and transportation may be different in different places. **Transportation** is the way people move from place to place.

These children live where it is cold. They like to play in the snow.

These children live where it is hot. They like to play in the water.

Some places farther north have green forests and mountains. People can go hiking or climbing. When it snows in the mountains, people can snowboard or ski.

Some places farther south have beaches. They are warm and sunny. Even in the winter, people can swim or surf in the ocean.

2 Find Evidence

Reread Why is outdoor fun sometimes different in different places?

Underline clues that support what you think.

3 Make Connections

Draw Make a picture that shows how you have fun where you live. Show what you do and what you wear.

Now draw a picture that shows how you would have fun in a different environment. How would your clothing and activity change?

Explore Cause and Effect

The **effect** is what happens.

The **cause** is why it happens.

To find the cause and effect:

1. Read the whole text.

2. Look for something that tells you what happens. This is an effect. Circle it.

3. Look for a detail that tells you why it happens. This is a cause. Underline it.

4. Ask yourself: *Did one thing make another thing happen?*

COLLABORATE Work with your class to complete the graphic organizer below.

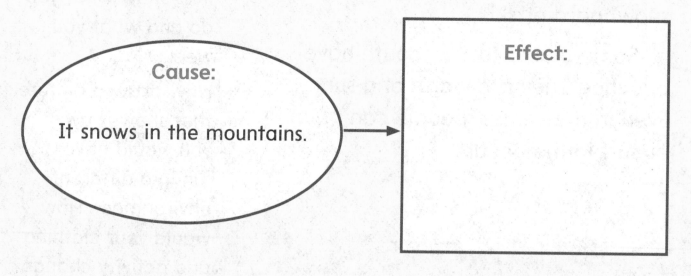

Cause:

It snows in the mountains.

Effect:

Investigate!

Read pages 78–85 in your Research Companion.

Look for details that tell you what happens and why it happens.

Write your information in the graphic organizer.

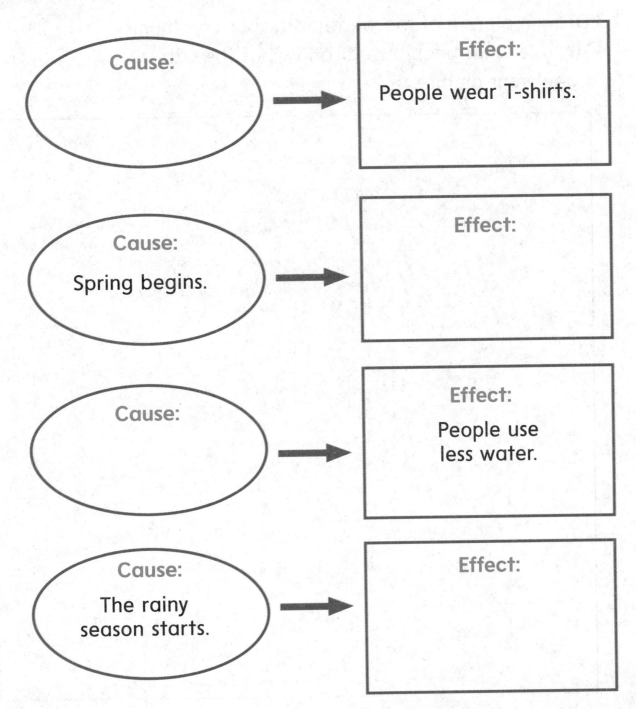

Cause:

Effect:
People wear T-shirts.

Cause:
Spring begins.

Effect:

Cause:

Effect:
People use less water.

Cause:
The rainy season starts.

Effect:

Think About It

What is the weather like in your community?
How does it change?

Draw It

Draw a picture of the weather in your community.
Include what people wear and what they do.
Label your picture.

Talk About It

Share your drawing with a partner. Together, talk about how location, weather, and environment affect your lives.

Connect to the EQ

Talk with a group. How do location and weather affect life in your community? Ask your teacher to make a list of your answers.

I. Location _____

_____

2. Weather _____

_____

3. Environment _____

_____

_____

How Can We Describe Where We Live?

Inquiry Project

Where We Live

In this project, you'll create a flipbook of different ways to describe where you live.

Complete Your Project

☐ Make your flipbook.

☐ Write one sentence on each page to tell where you live.

☐ Draw a picture for each page. It should show what makes the place special.

Share Your Project

☐ Read each sentence in your flipbook.

☐ Show the pictures that you drew. Explain why each place is special.

☐ Answer any questions your class might have.

Reflect on Your Project

Discuss with a partner what makes your community special.

Draw a picture of another way to describe where you live. Write a sentence to explain your picture.

Chapter Connections

Think back over this chapter. Tell a partner two different things you learned about how to describe where you live.

Country Cousin, City Cousin

CHARACTERS

City Cousin
Country Cousin
Taxi Cabs
Fruit Seller
Owls
Frogs
Narrator

Narrator: City Cousin liked the sounds of the city.

Taxi Cabs: Honk! Beep! ZOOM!

City Cousin: I also like buying fruit on the street.

Fruit Seller: Apples for sale! Oranges for sale! Bananas for sale!

City Cousin: I like the city. But I need a break.

Narrator: City Cousin knew just where to go. He got on a train and went to see Country Cousin.

Country Cousin: Hi! I live in the country. I like big fields and quiet rivers. Sometimes I hear owls and frogs at night.

Owls: Hoot, hoot!

Frogs: Ribbet! Ribbet!

Country Cousin: I like playing in the woods. I can be as loud as I want.

Narrator: Country Cousin picked up City Cousin at the train station.

City Cousin: Hi Cousin! It is good to see you. I need a break from city life.

Country Cousin: Well, let's go for a walk and enjoy the quiet!

Narrator: The cousins walked down a country lane. It was very quiet.

Owls: Hoot, hoot, HOOT!!!

City Cousin: What was that?!

Country Cousin: It was only an owl. I like the sound of hooting owls.

City Cousin: We don't have owls where I live. I'm not used to that sound.

Narrator: They kept walking. City Cousin was a little scared.

Frogs: Ribbet! RIBBET!

City Cousin: What was that?!

Country Cousin: It's just some frogs.

City Cousin: I thought it would be quiet here in the country.

Country Cousin: Well, we have our own sounds.

City Cousin: Yes, and it's still quieter than the city.

Country Cousin: Come on, Cousin. Let's get something to eat!

City Cousin: Sure! But where are all the people selling fruit?

Country Cousin: In the country, we pick our own fruit.

Narrator: The cousins stopped at an apple tree. They picked armfuls of apples. They went home and made a pie for dessert.

City Cousin: That pie was tasty! I like life in the country.

Country Cousin: I'll visit you in the city next time. You can take me for a taxicab ride!

How Do We Celebrate Our Country?

In this chapter, you'll explore how we celebrate our country. You'll read about how Americans remember important events and people from America's history. You'll also make a book of how we celebrate America!

Talk About It

COLLABORATE

Talk with your partner about how you celebrate America. What does America stand for?

Inquiry Project

My Book of Celebrating America

Work with your group to create your own book of symbols. Decide which symbols best celebrate and honor our country and your state. The symbols can be objects, places, or holidays.

Project Checklist

☐ Talk with your group about how we celebrate America and your state. Why do we celebrate them?

☐ Choose your favorite three symbols that celebrate America.

☐ Choose one favorite symbol that celebrates your state. .

☐ Make your own book.

☐ Write one sentence on each page to describe the symbol.

☐ Draw a picture for each symbol. Show as many details as you can.

My Research Ideas

What questions do you have about the project?

1. _____

_____

2. _____

_____

Explore Words

Complete this chapter's Word Rater. Write notes as you learn more about each word.

amendment   My Notes
- ☐ Know It!   _____
- ☐ Heard It!
- ☐ Don't Know It!   _____

celebrate   My Notes
- ☐ Know It!   _____
- ☐ Heard It!
- ☐ Don't Know It!   _____

colony   My Notes
- ☐ Know It!   _____
- ☐ Heard It!
- ☐ Don't Know It!   _____

document   My Notes
- ☐ Know It!   _____
- ☐ Heard It!
- ☐ Don't Know It!   _____

equality   My Notes
- ☐ Know It!   _____
- ☐ Heard It!
- ☐ Don't Know It!   _____

government   My Notes

☐ Know It!   _____

☐ Heard It!

☐ Don't Know It! _____

holiday   My Notes

☐ Know It!   _____

☐ Heard It!

☐ Don't Know It! _____

independence   My Notes

☐ Know It!   _____

☐ Heard It!

☐ Don't Know It! _____

monument   My Notes

☐ Know It!   _____

☐ Heard It!

☐ Don't Know It! _____

Why Do Americans Celebrate Independence Day?

Lesson Outcomes

What Am I Learning?

You will find out why Americans celebrate Independence Day.

Why Am I Learning It?

You will understand why Independence Day is an important holiday.

How Will I Know that I Learned It?

You will write and tell others about Independence Day and why we celebrate it.

Talk About It

COLLABORATE

Look closely at the picture. What do you think these men are doing? When did this happen? How do you know?

The founders signed the Declaration of Independence in 1776.

1 Inspect

Read Look at the title and captions. What do you think this text will be about?

Circle words you don't know.

Underline words that tell you:

- which country ruled the colonies.
- who made laws for the people in the colonies.
- what the colonists wanted.

My Notes

_____

_____

_____

The Thirteen Colonies

The United States began as a group of colonies. A **colony** is a place that belongs to a different country. England ruled the colonies. The King of England made the laws for the people who lived there.

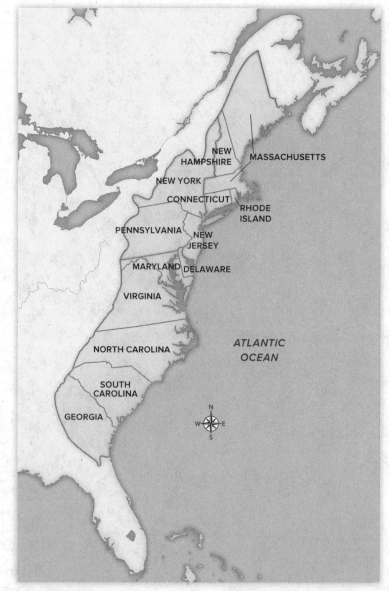

Long ago, England ruled the 13 colonies.

Leaders talked with colonists about how to gain independence from England.

The King of England made choices for the people in the colonies. They did not have the same rights as the people in England.

Many colonists were unhappy. They wanted to make their own laws. Leaders in the colonies discussed **independence**. Independence is being free to make your own choices.

Copyright © McGraw-Hill Education

2 Find Evidence

Reread Why were many colonists unhappy?

Underline clues that explain what the colonists didn't like.

3 Make Connections

Talk What did the colonists want to change? How do you think talking to each other helped?

Explore Sequence

Sequence is the order in which things happen.

To find the **sequence**:

1. Read the whole text.

2. Find out what happened first.

3. Look for what happened next and after that.

4. Find out what happened last.

Ask yourself: *Did I find the important things that happened? Can I retell them in the right order?*

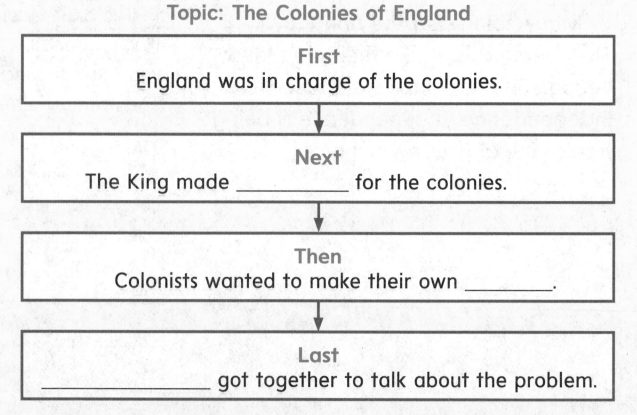 Work with your class to complete **COLLABORATE** the graphic organizer below.

Topic: The Colonies of England

First England was in charge of the colonies.

↓

Next The King made _____ for the colonies.

↓

Then Colonists wanted to make their own _____.

↓

Last _____ got together to talk about the problem.

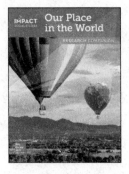

Investigate!

Read pages 96–101 in your Research Companion.

Look for details that tell you the order in which things happened.

Write your information in the graphic organizer.

Topic: How Independence Day Became a Holiday

> **First**
> Leaders wrote the _____.

> **Next**
> The colonies and _____ went to war.

> **Next**
> The colonies became _____.

> **Last**
> Independence Day is a holiday to celebrate _____.

Think About It

Think about what you have read. What makes Independence Day a special holiday for Americans?

Write About It

What is independence?

_____

_____

Why did the colonists want independence?
Use information from the text to explain.

_____

_____

_____

_____

Talk About It

Share your thoughts with a partner.
Discuss why we celebrate Independence Day.

Civics ## Connect to the

Pretend you have a pen pal who lives in another country. Write to your pen pal. Tell your pen pal how and why we celebrate Independence Day.

_____

_____

_____

_____

_____

_____

How Does the Constitution Help Our Country?

Lesson Outcomes

What Am I Learning?

You will learn about how the United States government works.

Why Am I Learning It?

You will be able to tell why the Constitution is important.

How Will I Know that I Learned It?

You will be able to explain how the Constitution helps our country.

Talk About It COLLABORATE

Read the words at the top of the Constitution. What do they say? Why do you think the Constitution begins with these words?

The pages of the
Constitution are on display
in Washington, D.C.

1 Inspect

Read Look at the title. What do you think this lesson will be about?

Circle words you don't know.

Underline clues that tell you:

- what the Constitution is.
- who serves in the Congress.
- who makes sure laws are fair.

My Notes

_____

_____

_____

Three Branches of Government

Long ago, leaders wrote the Constitution. The Constitution is the set of rules that explains how the United States **government** works. A government is a group of people who makes decisions for a state or country.

The leaders created a government with three branches, or parts.

- Congress is a group of leaders from each state. They make laws.

- The president makes sure the laws are followed.

- The Supreme Court makes sure laws are fair and follow the Constitution.

The web shows the three branches of the United States government. All the branches must work together to make sure the government works well.

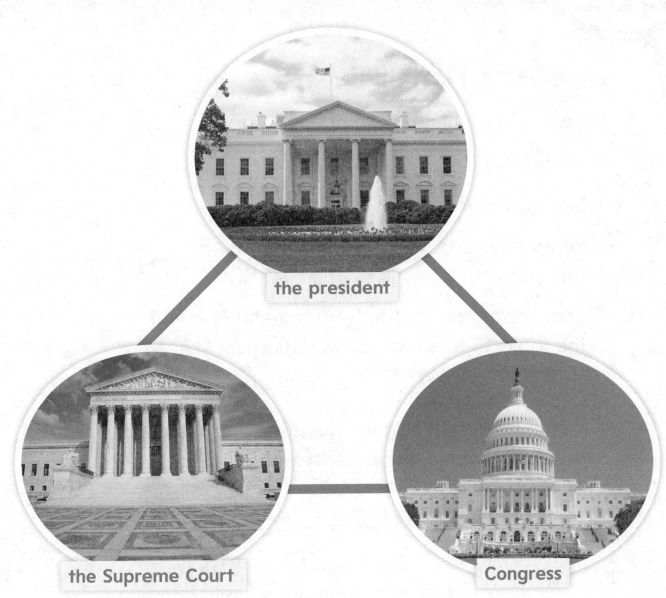

the president

the Supreme Court

Congress

2 Find Evidence

Reread How does the web help you understand the United States government?

Underline the job that each branch does.

3 Make Connections

Write What job does each branch of the United States government do?

Explore Details

Details give us information about the topic.

To find details:

I. Read the whole text.

2. Reread the text. What is it about? This is the topic.

3. Look for details that tell you something about the topic. Details may answer questions like *Who? What? When? Why?*

 Work with your class to complete the graphic organizer below.

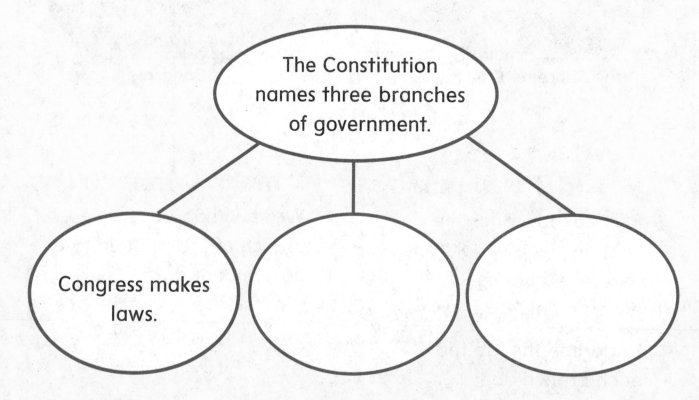

The Constitution names three branches of government.

Congress makes laws.

Investigate!

Read pages 102–107 in your Research Companion.

Look for details that tell you more about the government and the Constitution.

Write your information in the graphic organizer.

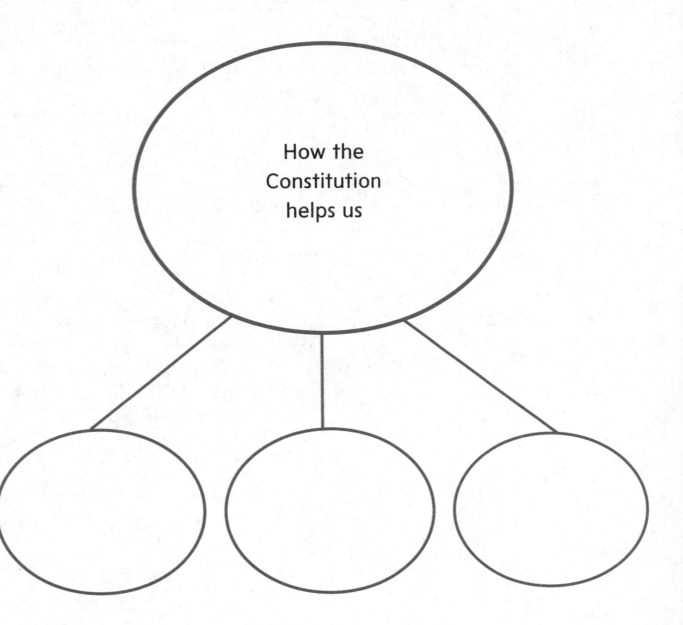

How the
Constitution
helps us

Think About It

Think about what you have read.
Why is the Constitution important?

Write About It

Complete the sentences.

1. The Constitution tells _____

_____

_____

_____

2. The Bill of Rights _____ people's rights.

3. _____ are changes to the Constitution.

Talk About It

Share your writing with your partner.
Discuss why the Constitution is important.

Connect to the EQ

izenship

What do you think our country would be like without the Constitution? Write one thing that would be different.

_____

_____

_____

Inquiry Project Notes

_____

_____

_____

Lesson 3

What Do Our National and State Symbols Mean?

Lesson Outcomes

What Am I Learning?
You will learn about the symbols that stand for our country and states.

Why Am I Learning It?
You will understand why we have symbols and what they mean.

How Will I Know that I Learned It?
You will draw and write about your favorite symbol of our country.

Talk About It

COLLABORATE

Look at the picture of the flag. This flag is a symbol that stands for something. What does it stand for?

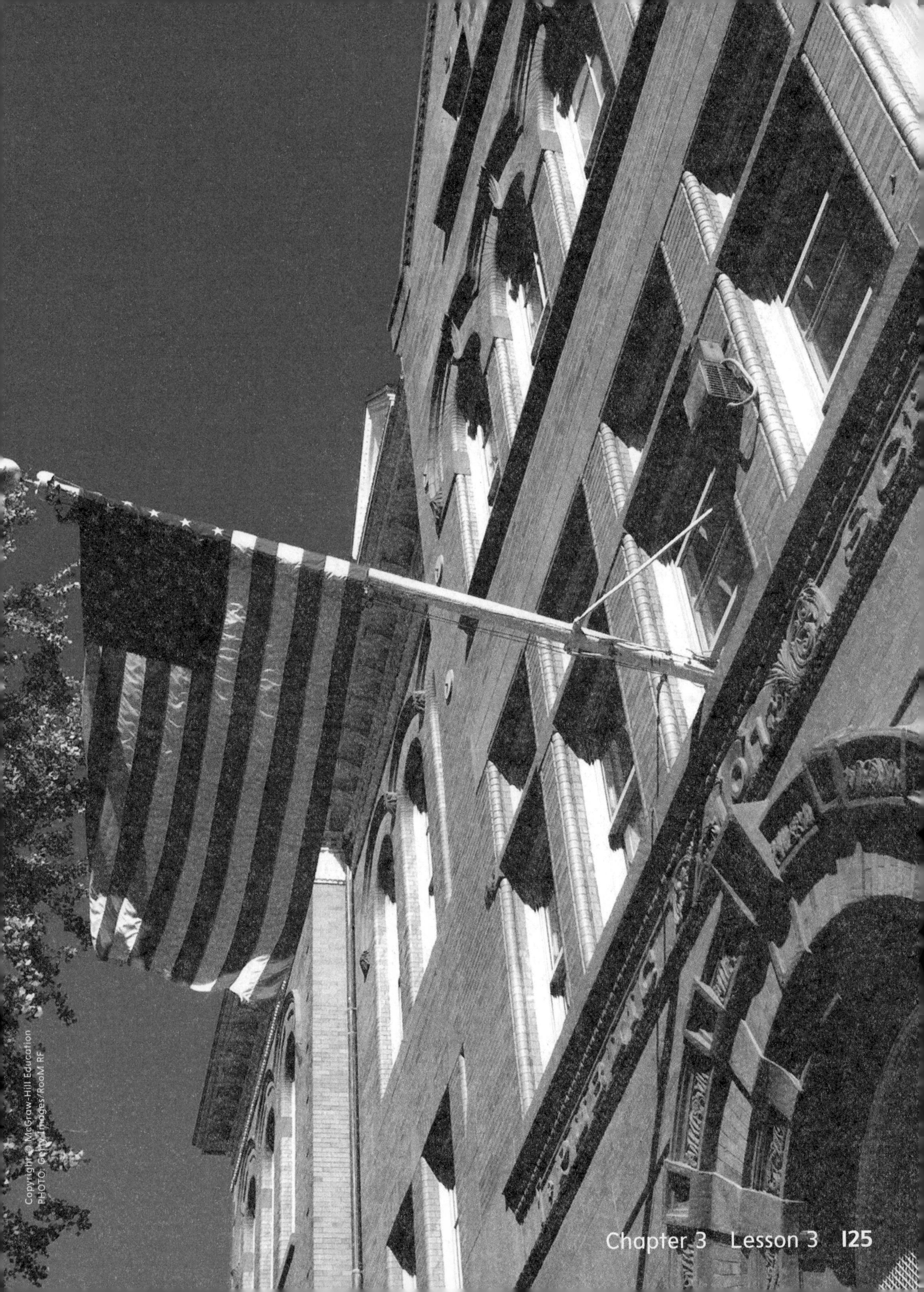

The American Flag

We honor the flag in many ways.

1 Inspect

Read Look at the titles and the picture caption. What do you think this text will be about?

Circle words you don't know.

Underline clues that tell you what the flag represents.

My Notes

_____

_____

_____

_____

You're a Grand Old Flag, Chorus

You're a grand old flag,

You're a high-flying flag,

And forever in peace
may you wave.

You're the emblem of
the land I love,

The home of the free
and the brave.

Ev'ry heart beats true

Under Red, White
and Blue,

Where there's never
a boast or brag.

But should auld acquaintance
be forgot,

Keep your eye on the
grand old flag.

The Pledge of Allegiance

I pledge allegiance
to the flag of the
United States of America,
and to the Republic for
which it stands,
one Nation under God,
indivisible,
with liberty and
justice for all.

These children are showing respect
for the flag.

2 Find Evidence

Talk What do you think the word *indivisible* means?

Reread the text.

Circle words that help you know the word's meaning.

3 Make Connections

Talk How does saying the Pledge of Allegiance or singing about the flag make you feel?

Explore Main Topic and Details

The **main topic** is what the text is about.

Details tell you more about the main topic.

To find the topic and details:

1. Read the title on each page. This is the topic of the text.

2. Read the text. Look for details that tell about the topic.

3. Look at the picture. Pictures can help show the topic or details of a text.

COLLABORATE Work with your class to complete the graphic organizer.

Symbol	What It Means
American flag	

Investigate!

Read pages 108–115 in your Research Companion.

Look for details about symbols.

Write your information in the graphic organizer.

Symbol	What It Means
	Our country gives freedom and hope.
Bald eagle	
	It tells something special about the state, like "Land of Lincoln" in Illinois.
State animal	

Think About It

Think about what you read. What symbols are important in the United States?

Write About It

Which symbol of our country is your favorite?
Draw a picture. Write why you like this symbol.

Talk About It

Share the symbol you chose with a partner.
Ask your partner about his or her symbol.

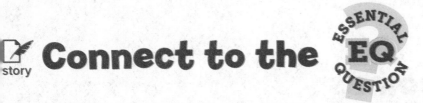

Connect to the

Find out about a symbol of your state. Write about it.

I. My symbol is _____

_____

2. It means _____

_____

3. It is important because _____

_____

What Do Monuments Help Us Remember?

Lesson Outcomes

What Am I Learning?
You will explore what monuments are and why they are important.

Why Am I Learning It?
You will understand why we have monuments and what they help us to remember.

How Will I Know that I Learned It?
You will draw a monument and write about it.

Talk About It   COLLABORATE

Look closely at the picture. What kind of building do you think this is? Why would people visit this building?

1 Inspect

Look at the map. What are some monuments and memorials you see?

Circle the monuments and memorials you see.

Highlight the names of the monuments and memorials you see.

My Notes

_____

_____

_____

_____

_____

Monuments and Memorials

Some buildings or statues are **monuments**. A monument is a building or statue that honors something or someone. We make monuments to help us remember important people and events.

Sometimes monuments are called memorials. Like monuments, memorials honor someone or a group of people. The Lincoln Memorial honors President Abraham Lincoln.

Did You Know?

There are monuments and memorials in every state in the United States.

Lincoln Memorial

Vietnam Veterans Memorial

World War II Memorial

Washington Monument

Martin Luther King, Jr. Memorial

National Mall in Washington, D.C.

Thomas Jefferson Memorial

The National Mall in Washington, D.C. has many monuments and memorials. They help us remember important people and events.

2 Find Evidence

Look closely again. Which monuments and memorials help us remember a person?

Which monuments and memorials help us remember an event?

How do you know? Use the details from the map to help you answer.

3 Make Connections

Talk Turn back to page 133.

Which president was the monument in the picture built for? Use the map to help you answer.

Explore Author's Purpose

The **author's purpose** is the reason why the author writes a text. To find the author's purpose:

I. Read and look for text details. Details are clues.

2. Ask yourself, *Why did the author write the text?*

Work with your class to complete the graphic organizer.

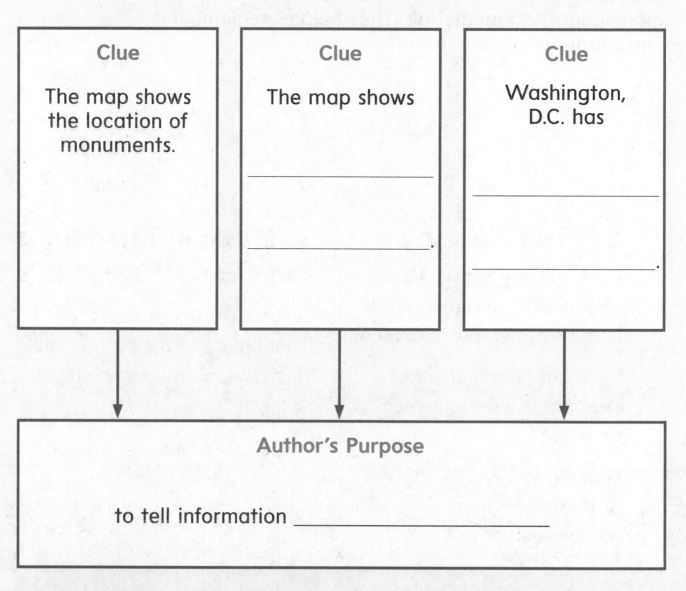

Clue	Clue	Clue
The map shows the location of monuments.	The map shows _____ _____.	Washington, D.C. has _____ _____.

Author's Purpose

to tell information _____

Investigate!

Read pages 116–123 in your Research Companion.

Look for clues that tell you the author's purpose.

Write the clues in your graphic organizer.

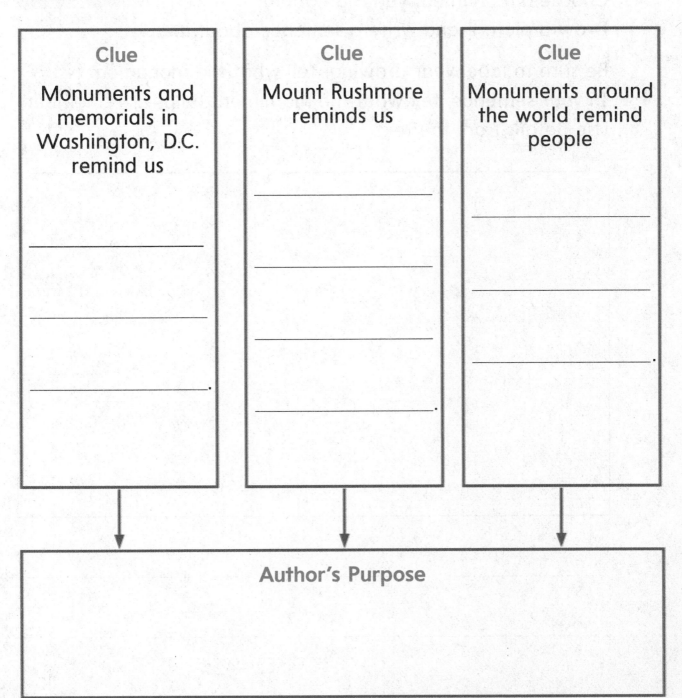

Clue	Clue	Clue
Monuments and memorials in Washington, D.C. remind us	Mount Rushmore reminds us	Monuments around the world remind people

Author's Purpose

Think About It

Think about your research. Why are monuments important?

Write About It

Choose a monument you read about.
Draw a picture and write a sentence about it.

Be sure to label your drawing. Tell what the monument is.
In your sentence, tell what the monument helps us remember.
Use details from the text.

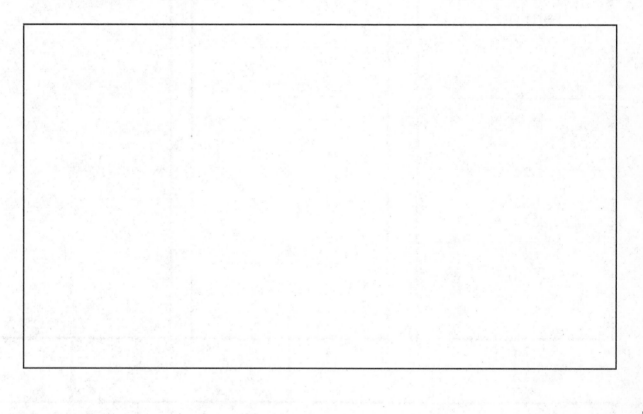

_____

_____

_____

Talk About It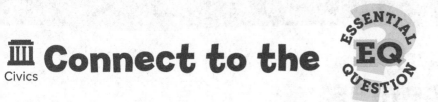

Share your work with a partner or a small group.
What new information did you learn?

Connect to the EQ

Civics

Which monument do you think would be the best to visit?
Write the name of the monument and two reasons.

_____

_____

_____

_____

_____

_____

_____

How Do We Celebrate Important People and Events?

Lesson Outcomes

What Am I Learning?

You will learn what it means to celebrate people and events.

Why Am I Learning It?

You will understand why we have holidays.

How Will I Know that I Learned It?

You will write an invitation to a holiday celebration.

Talk About It COLLABORATE

Look at the picture. What do you see on the front of the houses? Why do you think they are there?

People may fly flags to celebrate holidays.

1 Inspect

Read the title. What do you think this text will be about?

Circle the name of the holiday this text is about.

Underline words that tell you:

- when the holiday is.
- what the holiday was first called.
- what people do on this holiday.

My Notes

_____

_____

Memorial Day

The last Monday in May is Memorial Day. It is a day to remember American men and women who died in wars. We remember their service to our country. We feel proud of friends and family members who served.

Memorial Day was made a special day a long time ago. It was first called Decoration Day. It was a way to honor soldiers who died in the Civil War. Later, the name changed to Memorial Day.

Today, many communities have a parade on Memorial Day. The parade is to honor the soldiers. Some people visit monuments. They bring flags and flowers. People also fly the American flag on their homes and businesses.

We honor our soldiers with wreaths of flowers. This monument is in Arlington, Virginia. People visit it on Memorial Day.

2 Find Evidence

Reread Who does Memorial Day honor?

Underline the words that show you.

3 Make Connections

Talk Why do you think people fly the American flag on Memorial Day?

Explore Key Details

Key details help you understand a text.

To find key details:

1. Read the title. This is what the text is about. Circle the title.

2. Read the whole text.

3. Look for information that helps you understand the text. This is a key detail. Underline it.

COLLABORATE Work with your class to complete the chart below.

Holiday: Memorial Day	
Key Detail We remember soldiers who died in wars.	**Key Detail**

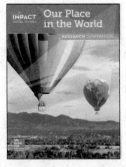

Investigate!

Read pages 124–129 in your Research Companion.

Look for details about holidays in your text.

Write the details in your graphic organizer.

Holiday: Veterans Day	Holiday: Martin Luther King, Jr., Day	Holiday: _____
Key Detail	Key Detail	Key Detail
Key Detail We have parades for the veterans.	Key Detail We can be kind to others.	Key Detail

Think About It

Think about what you read. How do we celebrate important people and events?

Write About It

Write an invitation to a holiday celebration.
Tell what, why, and how you are celebrating.

_____

_____

_____

_____

_____

_____

_____

Talk About It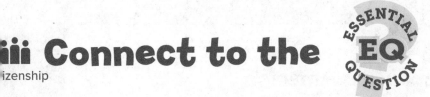

Share your invitation with a partner. Talk about why you chose that holiday.

Connect to the EQ

izenship

Which holiday do you think is the best celebration of our country? Use your notes from the graphic organizer to choose a holiday. Then complete the sentence.

_____ is the best celebration of

America because _____

_____.

Inquiry Project Notes

_____

_____

_____

Take Action

ESSENTIAL EQ QUES TIVES

How Do We Celebrate Our Country?

Inquiry Project

My Book of Celebrating America

For this project, you'll create a book of different symbols that celebrate America.

Complete Your Project

☐ Make your book.

☐ Write one sentence on each page to describe a different symbol.

☐ Draw a picture of the symbol on each page.

Share Your Project

☐ Read each sentence in your book.

☐ Show the pictures that you drew. Explain how each symbol celebrates America or your state.

☐ Answer any questions your class might have.

Reflect on Your Project

Discuss the project with a partner from another group. Did you include the same things in your books?

Draw a picture of another way to celebrate the United States. Write a sentence to explain your picture.

_____

_____

Chapter Connections

Think back over this chapter. Tell a partner two different things you learned about how we celebrate our country.

Past and Present

ESSENTIAL EQ QUESTION

How Does the Past Shape Our Lives?

In this chapter, you'll explore how the past has shaped our lives. You'll discover what life was like in the past and how it has changed or stayed the same. You will discover how many people and cultures make one nation. You'll also interview an adult to find out about one of their traditions. Then you'll make a poster about the tradition!

Talk About It   COLLABORATE

Talk with your partner about how the past is part of your life.

Copyright © McGraw-Hill Education
PHOTO: Bettmann/Getty Images

Inquiry Project

Sharing Traditions

Interview an adult in your family or from your community. Find out about a tradition that person knows about or has taken part in. Then create a poster to teach others about this tradition.

Project Checklist

☐ Think of an adult that you can interview.

☐ Brainstorm interview questions about the adult's tradition. Be sure to ask how the tradition has changed over time.

☐ Choose your favorite questions for the interview. You should have at least four questions.

☐ Interview the adult. Write down the answers.

☐ Create a poster about the tradition. Use pictures and words to explain what you learned.

My Research Ideas

List two people you might be able to interview.

1. _____

2. _____

Complete this chapter's Word Rater. Write notes as you learn more about each word.

culture   My Notes

☐ Know It!   _____
☐ Heard It!
☐ Don't Know It!   _____

                                _____

custom   My Notes

☐ Know It!   _____
☐ Heard It!
☐ Don't Know It!   _____

                                _____

history   My Notes

☐ Know It!   _____
☐ Heard It!
☐ Don't Know It!   _____

                                _____

interview   My Notes

☐ Know It!   _____
☐ Heard It!
☐ Don't Know It!   _____

                                _____

invent

My Notes

☐ Know It!

☐ Heard It! _____

☐ Don't Know It! _____

_____

present

My Notes

☐ Know It!

☐ Heard It! _____

☐ Don't Know It! _____

_____

tradition

My Notes

☐ Know It!

☐ Heard It! _____

☐ Don't Know It! _____

_____

How Can We Discover History?

Lesson Outcomes

What Am I Learning?
You will explore what we can learn from life long ago.

Why Am I Learning It?
You will learn how to explore your own community's past.

How Will I Know that I Learned It?
You will draw events from your own past.

Talk About It
COLLABORATE

Look closely at the time line. When was the girl born? When did she start school? What else do you see on the time line?

Look at some of the special things that have happened in this girl's life.

2012

2013

2014

2015

2016

2017

2018

Born

First Pet

First Day of School

Analyze the Source

Life Long Ago

The past can mean any time before now. It can mean yesterday. It can also mean a long time ago. There are many ways to learn about the past. One way is to look at photos taken long ago.

1 Inspect

Look at the photos.

Underline key details in the text.

Circle words that you don't know.

Take notes on the page. What is one way we learn about the past?

My Notes

_____

_____

_____

_____

_____

Long ago, some people built sod houses. Sod bricks are made from grass, roots, and dirt.

Old photos can tell you a lot about the past. Look at all the details in the photos. Think about life now. This is the **present**. What was different in the past?

This photo was taken long ago. Some toys are different today than they were in the past. Some toys are the same.

2 Find Evidence

Look Again How do the photos help you understand life long ago?

Discuss Look at the girls' clothes. How are clothes different now?

3 Make Connections

Talk Talk about life long ago. What is the same about life in the past and life today? What is different?

COLLABORATE

Turn back to page 155. How is the photo on this page like the photos on page 155?

Explore Key Details

A **key detail** tells you important information about the main topic.

The **main topic** is what a text is about.

I. Look for key details in the text.

2. Look for key details in photos and charts.

COLLABORATE Work with your class to complete the graphic organizer.

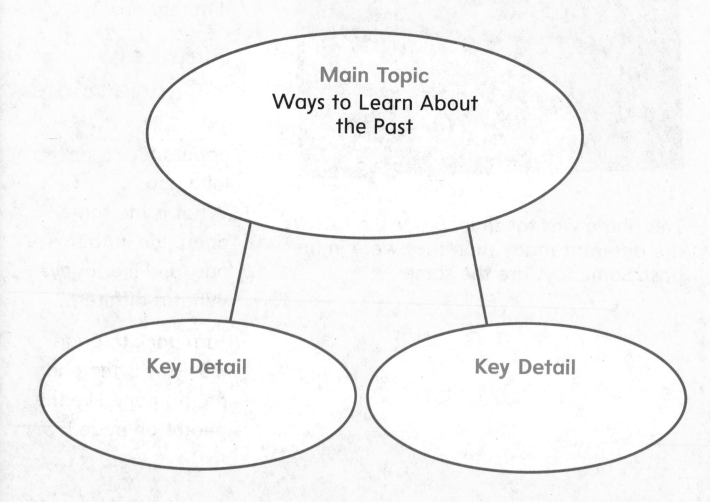

Main Topic
Ways to Learn About
the Past

Key Detail

Key Detail

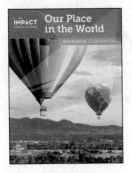

Investigate!

Read pages 140-145 in your Research Companion.

Look for key details related to the main topic.

Write the key details in the graphic organizer.

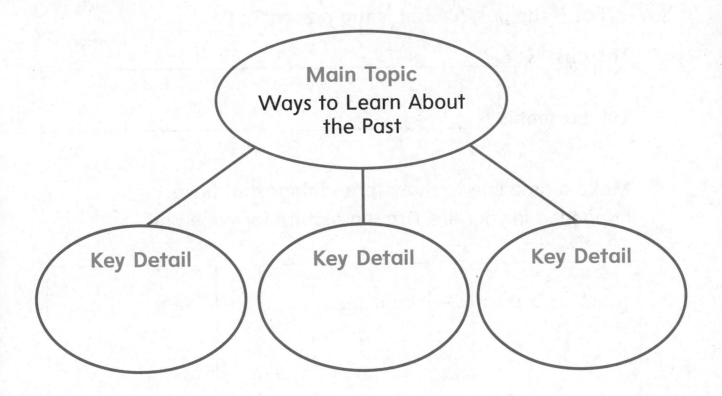

Main Topic
Ways to Learn About the Past

Key Detail

Key Detail

Key Detail

Think About It

Think about what you have learned. What is the past?
How do we learn about it?

Write About It

What is the past? What is the present?

The past is _____.

The present is _____.

Make a time line to show three things that have
happened in your life. Draw a picture for each one.

Year:_____   Year:_____   Year:_____

Talk About It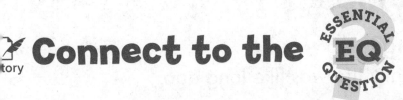

Share your time line with a partner.
What important events did you include?
How did you know about them?

Connect to the EQ

Imagine you want to learn about your community in the past. What would you do to find out about it? Where would you go? Who would you ask?

1. _____

_____

2. _____

_____

3. _____

_____

Lesson Outcomes

What Am I Learning?

You will explore what daily life was like long ago.

Why Am I Learning It?

You will understand how daily life has changed.

How Will I Know that I Learned It?

You will be able to tell how daily life today and long ago are the same and different.

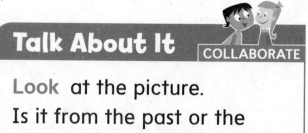

Talk About It   COLLABORATE

Look at the picture.
Is it from the past or the
present? How do you know?

Two Classrooms

1 Inspect

Look closely at the photos.

Take notes on the page. Write down questions you have about the photos.

2 Find Evidence

Look Again How have the classrooms stayed the same? How have they changed?

Circle the things that are the same in each picture.

Draw an arrow to point to the things that are different in each picture.

This is a classroom from long ago.

This is a classroom today.

3 Make Connections

Write What would you ask the students from long ago? Write one question.

Explore Compare and Contrast

When you **compare** two things, you think about how they are alike.

When you **contrast** two things, you think about how they are different.

To compare and contrast:

I. Study the two pictures.

2. Look for things that are alike.

3. Now look for things that are different.

COLLABORATE

Work with your class to complete the graphic organizer.

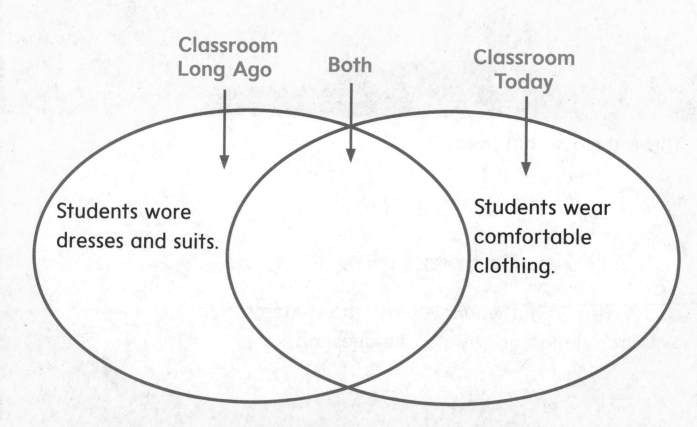

Classroom Long Ago   Both   Classroom Today

Students wore dresses and suits.

Students wear comfortable clothing.

Investigate!

Read pages 146–153 in your Research Companion.

Look for details about how life long ago and today are the same and different.

Write your information in the graphic organizer.

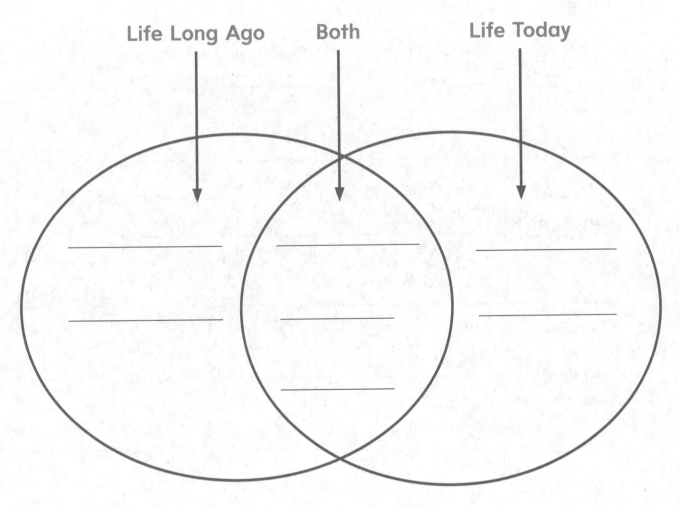

Life Long Ago   Both   Life Today

Think About It

Think about what you read. How is life now
the same as it was long ago? How is it different?

Write About It

Write one sentence to tell how daily life now is like it was in
the past. Write one sentence to tell how daily life is different.

Alike: _____

_____

_____

Different: _____

_____

_____

_____

_____

Talk About It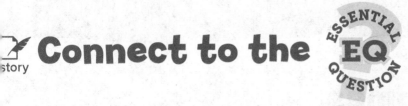

Share your sentences with a partner.
Talk about ways life has changed from the past.

Connect to the EQ

ESSENTIAL QUESTION

Imagine it is the first day of school long ago.
With a partner, list the things you might do to go
to school and at school. Then list the things you do today.

A School Day	
Then	Now

Lesson Outcomes

What Am I Learning?

You will learn about different cultures in the United States and around the world.

Why Am I Learning It?

You will be able to explain how cultures are alike and different.

How Will I Know that I Learned It?

You will draw and label something from your culture.

Talk About It COLLABORATE

Look closely at the picture. Tell about the children.

1 Inspect

Read Look at the title. What do you think this text will be about?

Circle words you don't know.

Underline clues that tell you:

- something all people do.
- who helped build the United States.
- where kindergarten came from.

My Notes

_____

_____

_____

One Country, Many Cultures

People all around the world do many of the same things. People eat. They work. They play. People also do some things differently. The special ways that people do things is called **culture**. The languages people speak are part of their culture. Their foods, songs, and games are, too.

The United States was made by people from many cultures. Native Americans lived here long before anyone else. Explorers and colonists came. Enslaved people were brought here. Immigrants from many places moved here. They shared their special ways to do things. They all helped build our country.

Did you go to kindergarten? People from Germany brought the idea here over 150 years ago. Today most children in the United States go to kindergarten. Do you jump rope? Dutch people brought jump ropes here long ago. Our country is full of great things from so many places!

Going to kindergarten is an idea that started in Germany long ago.

2 Find Evidence

Reread Why does the United States have things that come from other cultures?

Underline clues that tell you.

Discuss Why do people bring their culture with them when they move to a new place?

3 Make Connections

Talk What parts of your culture can you share with others?

COLLABORATE

Explore Summarizing

A **summary** is a short way to explain what you read.

To summarize:

1. Read the whole text. Look for important details.

2. Decide which details are important.

3. Tell all the important details in your own words.

COLLABORATE Work with your class to complete the graphic organizer.

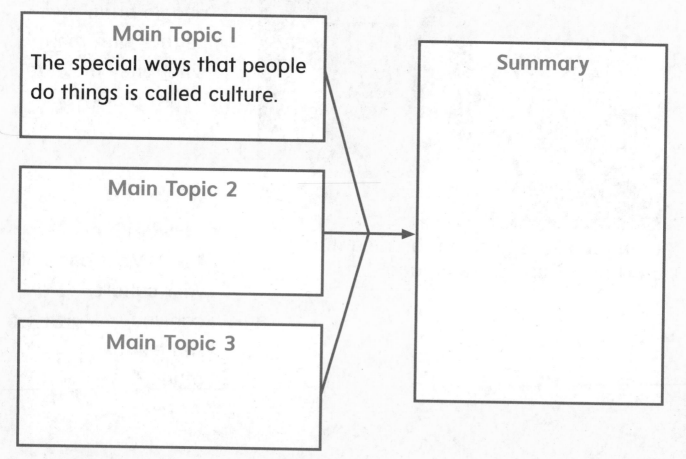

Main Topic 1
The special ways that people do things is called culture.

Main Topic 2

Main Topic 3

Summary

Investigate!

Read pages 154–161 in your Research Companion.

Look for the main ideas.

Write your notes to summarize the main ideas of what you read.

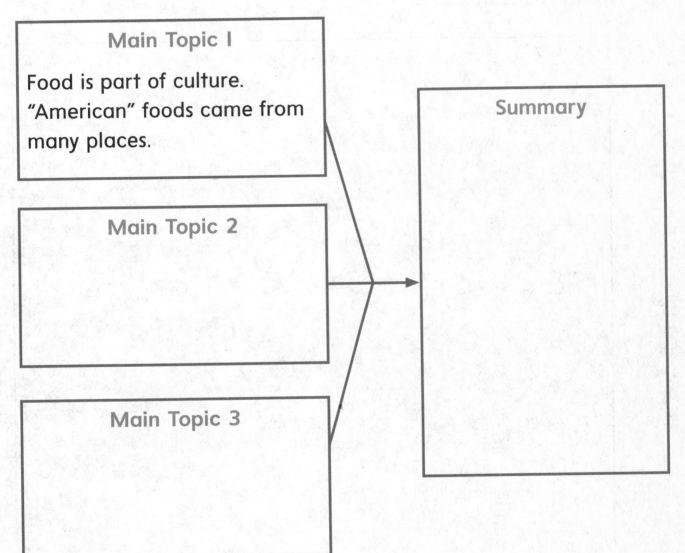

Main Topic 1

Food is part of culture. "American" foods came from many places.

Main Topic 2

Main Topic 3

Summary

Think About It

Think about what you have read. What is culture?

Draw It

Draw and label a picture that shows something from your culture.

Talk About It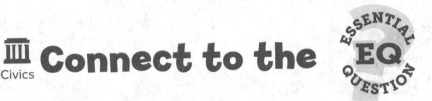

Share your picture with a partner. Explain your ideas, and answer your partner's questions about your drawing.

Civics

Connect to the EQ

What parts of different cultures can you find in the United States? Give examples based on what you know and what you read.

I. We eat foods _____

_____

2. Some of our sports and clothes _____

_____

3. We listen to _____

Inquiry Project Notes

_____

_____

What Are Customs?

Lesson Outcomes

What Am I Learning?
You will learn about different customs.

Why Am I Learning It?
You will be able to tell what customs are and describe some customs.

How Will I Know that I Learned It?
You will write about a custom.

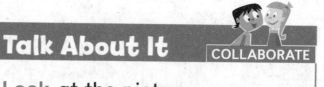

Talk About It
COLLABORATE

Look at the picture.
What are the people doing?
Where do you think they are?

Analyze the Source

1 Inspect

Look at the picture and title. What do you think you will learn?

Read the text.

Circle words you don't know.

Underline clues that tell you what the people are doing.

Take notes on the page.

My Notes

_____

_____

_____

_____

Celebrate!

Customs are things that a group of people do. Every culture has special customs. One kind of custom is when people celebrate. People celebrate important events, like family reunions or the New Year.

Other celebrations can be for:

- a wedding
- a graduation
- a new baby

Some people from Latin countries and cultures celebrate with a Quinceañera. Say it like this: _Kin-sin-nyair-a_. It is a birthday party for a 15-year-old girl. Families bring special kinds of food. They dance to music and eat a special cake.

Celebrations are fun!

A family celebrates a Quinceañera. A Quinceañera is a custom that comes from Mexico and other Latin countries.

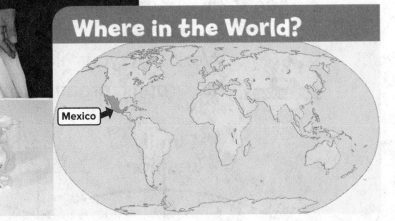

Where in the World?

Mexico

2 Find Evidence

Talk Why do people have a Quinceañera?

3 Make Connections

Talk The word *Quinceañera* comes from the Spanish words for "15" and "years." What does this tell you about the celebration?

COLLABORATE

Explore Compare and Contrast

When you **compare**, you show how things are alike.

When you **contrast**, you show how things are different.

To compare and contrast:

1. Read the whole text. It is about celebrations.

2. Think about two celebrations. How are they the same?

3. Then think about how they are different.

COLLABORATE Work with your class to complete the graphic organizer below.

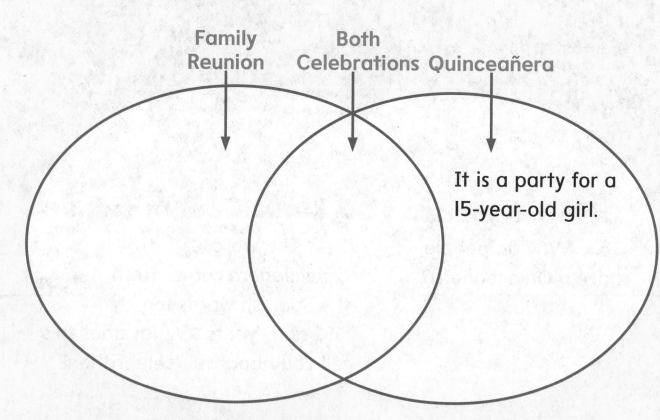

Family Reunion   Both Celebrations   Quinceañera

It is a party for a 15-year-old girl.

Investigate!

Read pages 162–167 in your Research Companion.

Look for details about two holidays people celebrate and how they are alike and different.

Write about the holidays in the graphic organizer.

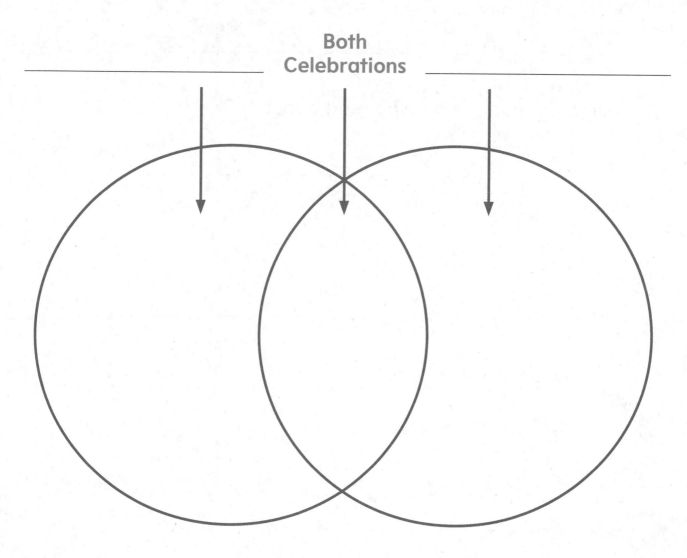

Both
Celebrations

Think About It

Think about what you read. What are customs?

Write About It

What is a custom?

A custom is _____

_____ .

Describe one custom you read about.

_____

_____

_____

_____

_____

Talk About It

Share your answers with a partner.
What details can you add?

Connect to the

EQ

ESSENTIAL QUESTION

Tell about three ways people in your community celebrate their customs.

1. Some people _____

_____.

2. Some people _____

_____.

3. Some people _____

_____.

Lesson 5

How Do Traditions Bring Us Together?

Lesson Outcomes

What Am I Learning?

You will learn what traditions are and how they bring people together.

Why Am I Learning It?

You will understand how traditions bring your family or community together.

How Will I Know that I Learned It?

You will write about traditions in your family and community.

Talk About It
COLLABORATE

Look closely at the photo. When was this photo taken? Do you have a dinner like this in your own family or community?

PRIMARY SOURCE

Marjory Collins was a photographer and writer. She took this photo long ago. It shows people enjoying a special dinner. This dinner is a tradition.

Traditions We Share

1 Inspect

Read the title. What do you think this text will be about?

Circle words you don't know.

Underline clues that will help you answer:

- What is a tradition?
- What is an example of a tradition?
- Why are traditions important?

Take notes on the page.

My Notes

_____

_____

A **tradition** is a way of doing something. It is handed down over the years. The photo on page 187 shows people eating a Thanksgiving meal. That is a tradition in the United States. People have Thanksgiving dinner every year at the same time of year.

Another tradition in our country is saying the Pledge of Allegiance. We put our hands on our hearts. Next, we look at the American flag. Then we say the words of the pledge. In many schools, children say the pledge every morning.

Traditions bring us together. They help us feel like part of a group. We may come from different places. We may have different ways. Traditions are something we can all share.

In some schools, students and teachers begin their day by saying the Pledge of Allegiance.

2 Find Evidence

Reread How do the text and photo show that traditions bring people together?

Circle clues in the text and photo that support what you think.

3 Make Connections

Talk Why do you think people enjoy traditions?

COLLABORATE

Explore Author's Purpose

The **author's purpose** is the reason why the author writes a text.

To find an author's purpose:

1. Read the text carefully.

2. Look for details that show why the author may have written the text. Details are clues to an author's purpose.

3. Ask yourself, *Why did the author write the text?*

COLLABORATE

Work with your class to complete the graphic organizer.

Detail
A tradition is a way of doing something that is handed down over the years.

↓

Author's Purpose

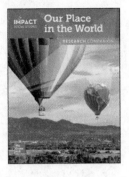

Investigate!

Read pages 168–173 in your Research Companion.

Look for details that help you understand the author's purpose.

Write the details in your graphic organizer.

Details
People can have differences but can share some things too.

↓

Author's Purpose

Think About It

Think about what you read. What kinds of traditions do people share?

Write About It

List three traditions in your family or community.

1. _____

_____

2. _____

_____

3. _____

_____

Talk About It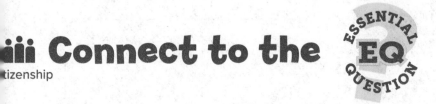

Share your list with your partner. How are your lists the same? How are they different?

Connect to the EQ

ESSENTIAL EQ QUESTION

Citizenship

What did you learn about your partner's traditions? Write what you learned and what you would like to know more about.

I learned _____

_____

_____

I would like to know more about _____

_____

_____

ESSENTIAL EQ QUESTION

How Does the Past Shape Our Lives?

Inquiry Project

Sharing Traditions

For this project, you will interview an adult to find out about a tradition and how it has changed or stayed the same. Then, you'll make a poster to show and tell about the tradition.

Complete Your Project

☐ Write your interview questions. Leave space for answers.

☐ Interview the adult about the tradition. Write the answers.

☐ Create your poster.

☐ Use pictures and words to share what you learned.

Share Your Project

☐ Tell who you interviewed.

☐ Tell about the tradition. Explain if it is the same or different from the past.

☐ Show your poster. Explain each part.

☐ Answer any questions your class might have.

Reflect on Your Project

Discuss with a partner different traditions people have. How do traditions help people celebrate their cultures?

Draw a picture of another tradition you or someone you know has. Write a sentence to explain your picture.

_____

_____

Chapter Connections

Think back over this chapter. Tell a partner two different ways the past shapes your life today.

Welcome to the Neighborhood!

CHARACTERS

Alec, from Greece   **Camila,** from Puerto Rico

Luca, from Italy   **Dora's Papa**

Dora, from Poland   **Narrator**

Narrator: It is the year 1915. Many people have immigrated to New York City. Dora is from Poland. Her family owns a fruit stand.

Dora's Papa: I need to go to the shoemaker. Mind the fruit stand, Dora. *(Dora's Papa leaves.)*

Dora: I sure wish I wasn't working. I want to play stickball! *(Alec and Luca walk up.)*

Luca: Did someone say stickball?

Alec: We'll play with you, Dora!

Dora: I can't play. I have to mind the fruit stand. Besides, we need another person to play.

Luca: Can't you take a little break?

(Camila walks by. She looks shy and a little scared.)

Alec: Hey, maybe she can play.

Dora: I've never seen her before. She must be new.

Luca: Hey, you! You want to play stickball with us?

Camila: Sorry, I don't know much English. I'm from Puerto Rico. I'm new here.

Alec: That's okay. We're all from someplace else. Luca's family is from Italy. Dora's family is from Poland. And I'm from Greece.

Dora: Do you want to play stickball?

Camila: What is stickball? I don't know many American customs.

Alec: We can teach you! Then you can teach us something new.

Camila: I can show you how to cook plantains. It is a kind of fruit. What kind of food do you eat?

Alec: My mother makes pita. It is bread that is flat.

Luca: My father makes meatballs just like they do in Italy.

Dora: We make potato pancakes for special holidays.

Camila: Oh! That sounds good!

(Dora's Papa comes back.)

Dora's Papa: Hello. You must be with the new family down the street.

Camila: Yes, my name is Camila.

Dora: Camila eats a kind of fruit I never heard of. They are called plantains.

Dora's Papa: Hmm. Maybe we should sell them at the fruit stand.

Dora: And then we can sell them to Camila's family.

Dora's Papa: That's a good idea, Dora.

Alec: Hey, Dora. What about that game?

Luca: Yeah, we want to play!

Dora: Papa, may I go and play?

Dora's Papa: Yes, that's fine.

Alec: Hooray!

Luca: Finally!

Alec: All of this talk about food is making me hungry.

Luca: I was thinking of stickball. Now I'm thinking of meatballs!

Dora's Papa: That reminds me. Dora, be back in time for dinner.

Dora: I will. Hey! We should all have dinner to welcome Camila's family to the neighborhood.

Alec: I'll bring pita bread!

Luca: I'll bring meatballs!

Camila: I'll bring plantains!

Dora's Papa: You see, Camila? In America, we say "Welcome" with food!

All: The end.

ESSENTIAL EQ QUESTION

Why Do People Work?

In this chapter, you'll learn why people work. You'll learn about trading and what it means to make money. You will also learn the difference between wants and needs. At the end of the chapter, you'll create a market in the classroom. You will pretend to trade or purchase goods and services with your classmates!

Talk About It COLLABORATE

Talk with your partner about the jobs people do. What questions do you have about why people work?

Inquiry Project

Classroom Market

Work in groups to make a classroom market. Think about what a market is like and what you might find there. Trade, buy, and sell goods and services.

Project Checklist

☐ Brainstorm with your class what will be sold in each group's market area. What goods will you make? What services will you provide?

☐ Discuss rules for the market. What rules will you follow to be fair? What rules can you follow to get along?

☐ Choose one good or service for each person in your group to sell.

☐ Create your good or make a sign for your service. Your teacher will provide you with the "money" you earned.

☐ Decide on a fair cost for your product.

☐ Sell your good or service on your class market day.

☐ Purchase goods and services that you would like.

My Research Ideas

What could you sell at a market?

1. _____

2. _____

Complete this chapter's Word Rater. Write notes as you learn more about each word.

consumer　　My Notes

☐ Know It!　　_____

☐ Heard It!　　_____

☐ Don't Know It!　_____

equipment　　My Notes

☐ Know It!　　_____

☐ Heard It!　　_____

☐ Don't Know It!　_____

goods　　My Notes

☐ Know It!　　_____

☐ Heard It!　　_____

☐ Don't Know It!　_____

needs　　My Notes

☐ Know It!　　_____

☐ Heard It!　　_____

☐ Don't Know It!　_____

producer　　My Notes

☐ Know It!　　_____

☐ Heard It!　　_____

☐ Don't Know It!　_____

scarcity   My Notes

☐ Know It!   _____

☐ Heard It!   _____

☐ Don't Know It!   _____

services   My Notes

☐ Know It!   _____

☐ Heard It!   _____

☐ Don't Know It!   _____

trade   My Notes

☐ Know It!   _____

☐ Heard It!   _____

☐ Don't Know It!   _____

volunteer   My Notes

☐ Know It!   _____

☐ Heard It!   _____

☐ Don't Know It!   _____

wants   My Notes

☐ Know It!   _____

☐ Heard It!   _____

☐ Don't Know It!   _____

Lesson Outcomes

What Am I Learning?

You will learn about goods and services.

Why Am I Learning It?

You will understand why goods and services are important in your community.

How Will I Know that I Learned It?

You will show and explain the differences between goods and services.

Talk About It   COLLABORATE

Read the poem. What is one thing the poem tells you about goods? What is one thing the poem tells you about services?

Goods and Services

Goods are different things

That people make and use.

We can buy and sell

Any goods we choose.

Services are jobs or work

One person does for another.

We can buy or sell

Services to each other.

1 Inspect

Look at the title. What do you think this chart will show?

Circle two pictures of goods.

Underline two pictures of services.

My Notes

_____

_____

_____

_____

_____

Goods and Services

Goods

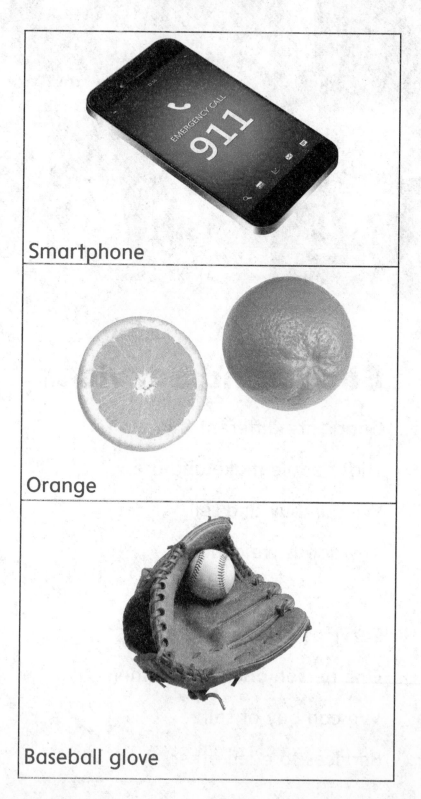

Smartphone

Orange

Baseball glove

Services

Dentist

Teacher

Server

2 Find Evidence

Reread Look at the chart. Who would help you in a restaurant?

3 Make Connections

Talk What goods do you use every day in school? What is an important service in your community?

COLLABORATE

Explore Key Details

Key details tell information about a main topic.

Use words and photos to help you find key details.

To find the key details:

1. Read the whole text.

2. Circle words that give bits of important information.

3. Look carefully at the photos. Look for helpful information.

COLLABORATE Work with your class to complete the graphic organizer.

Goods	Services
Orange	Dentist

Investigate!

Read pages 184–191 in your Research Companion.

Look for text evidence that tells you the key details about goods and services.

Write your information in the graphic organizer.

Goods	Services
Definition: things that people _____	Definition: work that people _____
bread	baker

Think About It

Think about your research.
Why do we need goods and services?

Write About It

What are goods and services?

Goods are _____

_____

Services are _____

_____

Name one good. Name one service. Tell how they are different.

_____

_____

_____

Talk About It

Tell your partner about your good and service.
Can he or she explain which is a good and which is
a service?

Connect to the

Which goods and services are important in your
community? Write an advertisement for one.
Tell whether it is for a good or a service.

_____

_____

_____

_____

_____

_____

Lesson Outcomes

What Am I Learning?
You will explore what trade is and how people trade with others.

Why Am I Learning It?
You will learn why and how people trade and why it is important.

How Will I Know that I Learned It?
You will write about trade and show how you can earn and spend money.

Talk About It
COLLABORATE

Look closely at the picture. What do you see? What are the children doing?

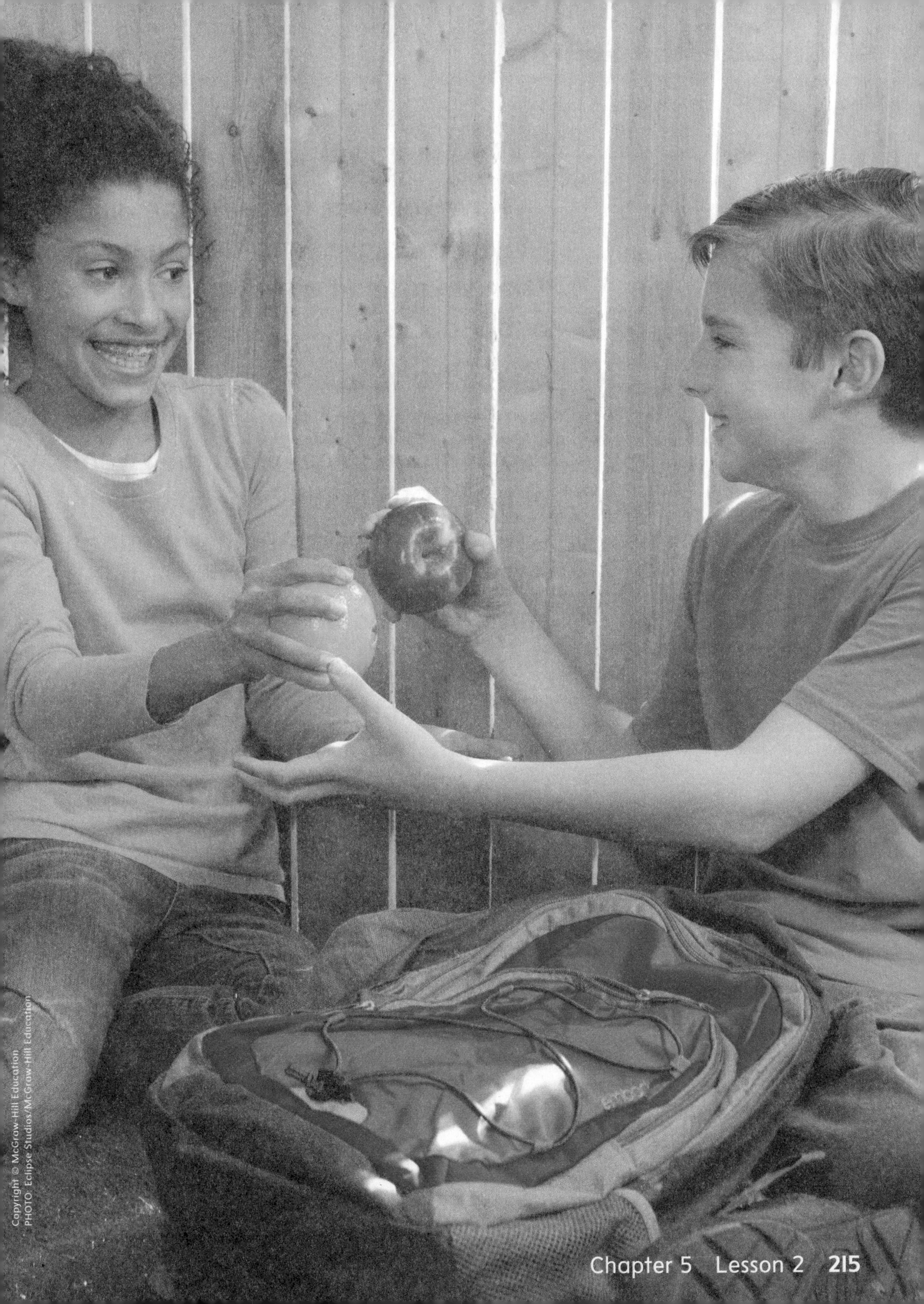

Look at the title and the pictures. What do you think this text will be about?

Circle words you don't know.

Underline clues that tell you:

- what trade is.
- what money is.

My Notes

_____

_____

_____

_____

Trade and Money

Have you ever traded something? Maybe you gave your friend a book. Then your friend gave you one of his or her books.

You **trade** when you give something to get something else. People trade to get what they want or need. One group of people might have a lot of food. Another group might have many tools. The groups can trade food and tools to get what they need.

Today most people use money to get things. Money is coins or paper bills. Money makes trading easy. People work to get money. They use money to buy goods.

People use money to buy things.

2 Find Evidence

Reread Why do people trade?

Underline the clues that help you answer.

3 Make Connections

Talk Turn back to page 215. Why are these children trading?

Explore Ask and Answer Questions

You can ask yourself questions about what you read.

This will help you think about the parts you do not understand.

Look in the text for answers to your questions.

 Work with your class to complete the graphic organizer.

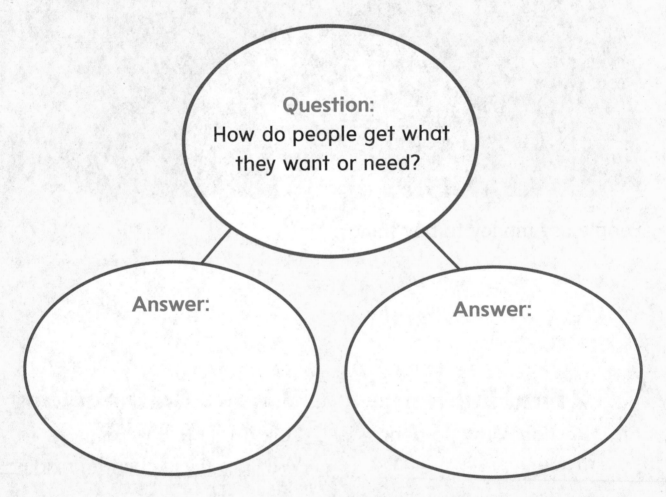

Question:
How do people get what they want or need?

Answer:

Answer:

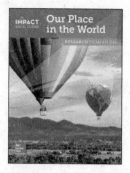

Investigate!

Read pages 192–197 in your Research Companion.

Look for details about how we get goods.

Write your information in the graphic organizer.

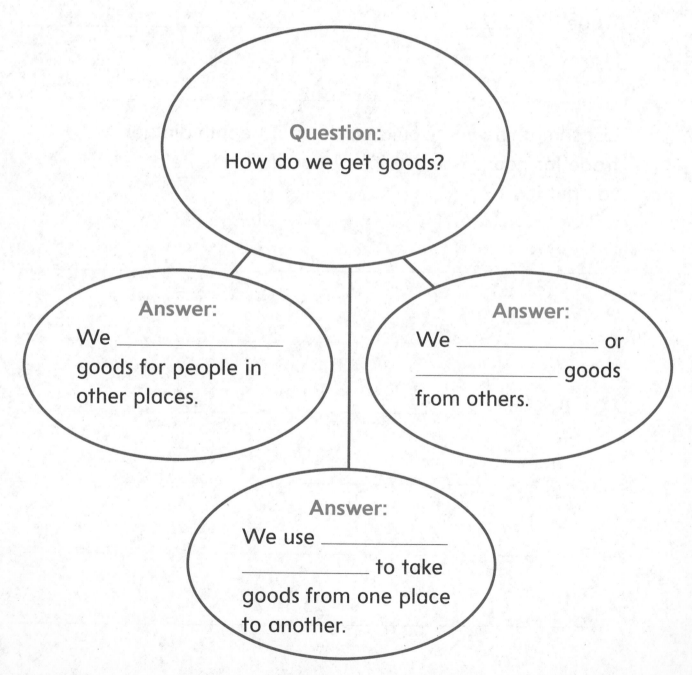

Question:
How do we get goods?

Answer:
We _____ goods for people in other places.

Answer:
We _____ or _____ goods from others.

Answer:
We use _____ _____ to take goods from one place to another.

Think About It

Think about what you learned. What does it mean to trade?

Write About It

Trade is _____

_____.

List something you would not have if people did not trade for goods and services. How did trade help you get it?

_____

_____

_____

_____

_____

_____

Talk About It

COLLABORATE

Share your writing with a partner. How does trade help you get goods and services?

Connect to the

Economics

Pretend you did a chore and earned money. Draw a picture of a good you would buy with the money you earned from working hard.

Lesson Outcomes

What Am I Learning?

You will learn what kinds of jobs people do.

Why Am I Learning It?

You will understand where people work and why we need the jobs people do.

How Will I Know that I Learned It?

You will write about different kinds of jobs.

Talk About It
COLLABORATE

Look at the picture. Where do you think this person works? What other work might this person do each day?

1 Inspect

Read the title. What do you think this text will be about?

Circle words you don't know.

Underline clues that tell you:

- why people have jobs.
- what kinds of jobs people can do.

My Notes

_____

_____

_____

Jobs

Most people have jobs. This is how people earn money. At a job, people are paid for their work. They trade work for money.

There are many kinds of jobs. Workers do things that help others. An office worker may help people solve problems. A factory worker makes goods that people use. A scientist works in a lab to discover new things.

Some office workers use computers at their jobs.

Crossing guards have the job
of keeping children safe.

There are other kinds of jobs, too. People work as teachers and farmers. They work as cooks and doctors.

Some people take care of places or animals. A park ranger takes care of a park. A zookeeper looks after animals. Those sound like fun jobs!

People make money at their jobs. They use money to buy things they want or need. Jobs are an important part of our world.

2 Find Evidence

Reread the text.

Underline the words that tell what people use their money for.

3 Make Connections

Talk What kinds of jobs do people do in your community?

COLLABORATE

Explore Fact and Opinion

A **fact** is a statement that is true all the time, no matter who is reading or saying it.

An **opinion** is what a person thinks or believes. Opinions can be different for different people.

 As you read the text, work with your class to complete the graphic organizer.

Fact	Opinion
People use money to get goods.	Jobs are an important part of our world.

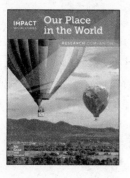

Investigate!

Read pages 198–205 in your Research Companion.

Look for details about the kinds of jobs that people do.

Write the details in your graphic organizer.

Fact	Opinion
Firefighters are always ready to protect people.	
	Volunteers are very important.
Jacob Lawrence was a painter.	

Think About It

Think about what you read. What kinds of jobs do people do?

Write About It

List three places where people can work.

1. _____

_____

_____

2. _____

_____

_____

3. _____

_____

_____

Talk About It

Share your responses with your partner.
Talk about what jobs you think you would like to do.

Connect to the EQ

Civics

Why do people work? Choose
one job and list three reasons why someone would work
at that job.

Job: _____

Reason # 1: _____

_____

Reason # 2: _____

_____

Reason # 3: _____

_____

Lesson Outcomes

What Am I Learning?

You will learn about work in the past and work today.

Why Am I Learning It?

You will be able to talk and write about how and why work has changed over time.

How Will I Know that I Learned It?

You will write about one job and how it was different in the past and what it is like today.

Talk About It

COLLABORATE

Look closely at the photo. What are the people doing?

What details in the photo help you learn about farming long ago?

Farming Then and Now

1 Inspect

Read Look at the title. What do you think this text will be about?

Underline words that tell how farmers did their work long ago.

Circle words that you don't understand.

My Notes

_____

_____

_____

_____

_____

Long ago, most of the people in the United States lived on farms. They produced their own food. They grew or raised it on their land. Farmers did work by hand or with horse-drawn **equipment**, or tools. They worked hard. They worked every day.

Today, most farms produce food for others to eat. Farmers use machines instead of horses. This equipment is faster. Farmers can grow more crops. They can raise more animals.

One thing is the same about farming long ago and today. Farm families work hard!

A "combine" machine helps to gather wheat on a farm today.

2 Find Evidence

Reread What do the text and the photos tell you about farm equipment?

Underline the words that tell what farmers can do with new equipment.

3 Make Connections

Talk Why is modern farm equipment faster than horse-drawn equipment?

Explore Make Connections

Making connections means using text and pictures together. They both show clues that can tell you about an important idea.

To make connections:

1. Read the text. Underline details that tell more about the important idea.

2. Look at the pictures. Circle the parts of the pictures that show clues about the idea.

3. Make connections between the text, the pictures, and the idea.

COLLABORATE Work with your class to complete the graphic organizer.

Text Details	Picture Clues	Idea
Farmers long ago used horses. Farmers today use machines.		Farming has changed in some ways.

Investigate!

Read pages 206–211 in your Research Companion.

Look for details in the text and pictures.

Write your information in the graphic organizer.

Text Details	Picture Clues	Idea
In the past, workers used equipvment like _____	Workers today use _____	Today, machines and computers make work _____
_____	_____	_____
_____	_____	_____
_____	_____	_____
_____	_____	_____
to get jobs done.	to get jobs done.	_____.

Think About It

Think about what you read. What is one way work has changed over time?

Write About It

Think about a job you might like to have when you grow up. What is one way this job might have been different in the past?

When I grow up, I would like to _____

_____

_____

_____.

In the past, this job might have been _____

because _____

_____

_____.

Talk About It

Share your job with a partner. Tell your partner what your job was like in the past. Tell what it is like today.

Connect to the

Choose a job you learned about. Write a dialogue between two characters that have that job. One character has the job in the past, and one has the job today. Have your characters tell each other how they work and what it is like to do that job.

_____

_____

_____

_____

_____

How Are Wants and Needs Different?

Lesson Outcomes

What Am I Learning?

You will explore the difference between needs and wants.

Why Am I Learning It?

You will understand what things people need and how they are different from things people want.

How Will I Know that I Learned It?

You will write about your own wants and needs.

Talk About It   COLLABORATE

Look at the picture. What do you think the children are doing? What details make you think so?

GAMES

1 Inspect

Look at the photos. What do you think is one answer to this question?

Underline key details in the text.

Circle words you don't know.

My Notes

_____

_____

_____

_____

_____

Why Do We Spend Money?

People need certain things to live. We need air, water, food, and clothes. We also need shelter. Shelter is a place to live. The things we need are necessary. That means we cannot live without them. Only air is free. The rest cost money.

We only have a certain amount of money. We have to make good choices about how we use our money. We should not use it to get only the things that we want. Then we may not have any left for the things we need.

Pretend you have some money to buy new pencils. But you decide to buy a toy and stickers first. Now you might not have enough money left for the pencils. It will be hard to do your math problems!

This girl wants a new bike.

Reread the text.

Circle information that tells about the things you need and the things you want.

3 Make Connections

Talk How do we choose what to buy? What kinds of things might this dad and daughter need to think about before they decide to buy a bike?

Explore Classify

When you **classify**, you put things that are alike into groups.

COLLABORATE As you read the text, work with your class to complete the graphic organizer.

Needs	Wants
air	
	toys

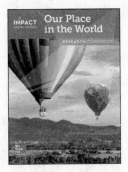

Investigate!

Read pages 212–217 in your Research Companion.

Look for details that help you classify needs and wants.

Write or draw your notes or pictures in this chart.

Needs	Wants
shelter	games

Think About It

Think about what you read.

What did you learn about wants and needs?

Write About It

What is the difference between a want and a need?

_____

_____

List one thing you need and one thing you want.

I need _____

_____

I want _____

_____

Talk About It

Talk with your partner. What is a thing your partner needs? What is a thing your partner wants? Did you list the same things?

Connect to the

Why do people have to make choices about money?

_____

_____

_____

_____

_____

_____

Why Do People Work?

Inquiry Project

Classroom Market

For this project, you will create a marketplace in your classroom. You will buy, trade, and sell goods and services.

Complete Your Project

☐ Decide on your good or service.

☐ Make your product or a sign telling about your service.

☐ Choose a price for your product.

Share Your Project

☐ Sell or trade your good or service. Describe what you are selling.

☐ Purchase goods and services from your classmates.

☐ Talk with your group about what you each bought.

Reflect on Your Project

Discuss the project with a partner. What did you like about producing, selling, and consuming?

Complete the sentences.

The best part of the market was _____

_____

If I could change something, I would _____

_____

I spent my money on _____ because _____

_____

Chapter Connections

Think about the chapter. Tell a partner the most interesting thing you learned.

Reference Sources

The Reference Section has a glossary of vocabulary words from the chapters in this book. Use this section to explore new vocabulary as you investigate and take action.

Glossary

A

address information that tells where a person lives

amendment an official change in the words or meaning of a law or document (such as a constitution)

B

border a line where one country or area ends and another begins

C

capital a city where the government of a country or state is located

celebrate to do something special or enjoyable for an important event, occasion, or holiday

citizen a person who is part of a group or lives in a particular place

colony an area that is controlled by or belongs to another country

community a group of people who live together in the same place

consumer someone who buys and uses goods or services

continent one of the seven large areas of land on Earth

culture the arts, beliefs, and customs of a particular group of people at a particular time

custom a way of acting that is usual among the people in a group

D

democracy a government that is run by the people who live under it

document an official paper that gives official information or proof about something

E

environment the natural world

equality the same rights for everyone

equipment supplies or tools needed for a special purpose

G

globe an object that is shaped like a large ball with a map of the world on it

goods things that people make, buy, and sell

government a group of people who control and make decisions for a country, state, city, or other place

H

history what happened in the past

holiday a special day to celebrate a person or event

I

independence freedom from the control of another or others

interview a meeting to get information from someone; a report based on an interview

invent to make or think of something for the first time

R3

L

law a rule made by the government of a town, state, or country

location a place where something can be found

M

monument a building, statue, or other object made to honor a person or event

N

needs things a person must have to live

neighborhood a small area in a town or city where people live

P

past a time that has gone by

present today or now

producer someone who grows or makes things to sell

R

respect a feeling or understanding that someone or something is important and should be treated in an appropriate way

responsibility something a person should do

rights things a person is free to do

scarcity when there is not enough of something

services work people do for someone else

symbol a picture that stands for something else

trade the activity or process of buying, selling, or exchanging goods or services

tradition a custom that has been performed by the people in a particular group for a long time

transportation the act or process of moving people or things from one place to another

volunteer a person who works without pay to help other people

voting expressing a wish by making a choice that is counted

W

wants things a person would like to have but does not need to live